Four Glorious Brothers

THe Chanukkah War
as told in the ancient
Sifrei Maccabim

by

Rabbi Pinchas Stolper
with
Rabbi Yaakov Lavon

ISBN 1-60091-001-7

First Edition, November 2006

Published by
David Dov Foundation
603 Twin Oaks Drive
Lakewood, NJ 08701

Distributed by
Israel Book Shop
501 Prospect St.
Lakewood, NJ 08701
Tel. 732-901-3990   Fax 732-901-4012
isrbkshp@aol.com

Copyright © 2006 by Pinchas Stolper, David Dov Foundation

All rights reserved. No part of this publication may be translated, reproduced, stored in a retrieval system or transmitted, in any form or by any means, electronic, photocopying, recording or otherwise, without prior permission in writing from the copyright holders, except by a reviewer who wishes to quote brief passages in connection with a review written for inclusion in magazines or newspapers. The rights of the copyright holders will be strictly enforced.

FIVE GLORIOUS BROTHERS

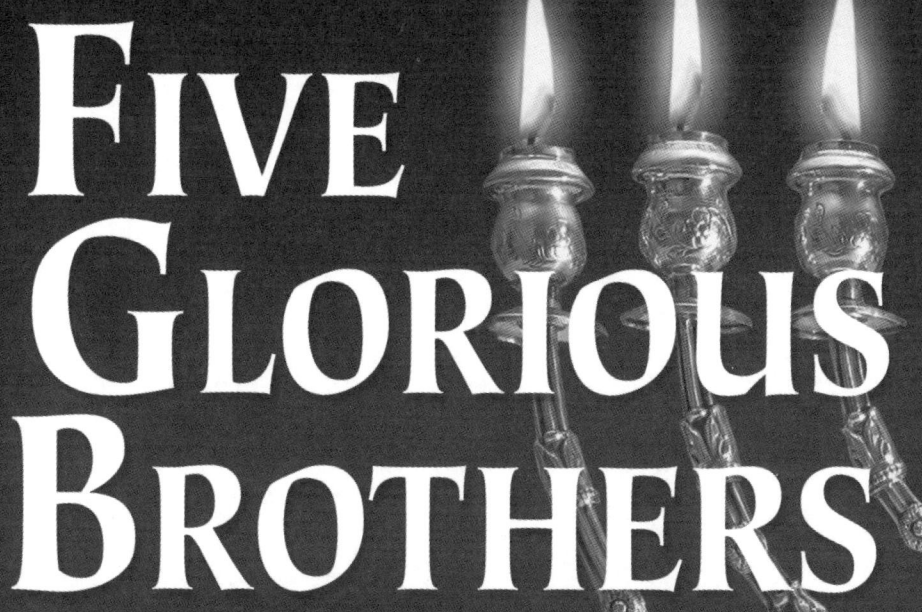

The Chanukah War as told in the Ancient Sifrei Maccabim

Rabbi
Pinchas
Stolper

with
Rabbi
Yaakov
Lavon

דוד קאהן　　　　　　　　　　　　ביהמ״ד גבול יעבץ
　　　　　　　　　　　　　　　　ברוקלין, נוא יארק

בס״ד

My dear friend, Rav Pinchos Stolper shlita, has embarked on a project to demonstrate the depth of Torah weltanschauung by utilizing his multi-faceted talents of originality and presentation. In his new sefer complex concepts become lucid, and winding paths become straight.

More power to him! May he continue to disseminate the Torah's wisdom for many years to come.

דוד קאהן
בלונ״ר דוד יוסף

Vaad L'Hatzolas Nidchei Yisroel

of Stam Gemilas Chesed Fund, Inc.   Tax Exempt #22-2371275
401 Yeshiva Lane • Baltimore, Maryland 21208 • Tel: 410-484-7396
Fax: 410-486-8810 • E-Mail: eisemann@erols.com
In order to be received, all e-mails must contain
the word "Kashor" within the Subject line

Rabbi Moshe M. Eisemann

July 12, 2006

Dear R' Pinchos:

I have always felt that one of the greatest miracles of Chanukah is that year after year people find and explore new, as yet untrodden paths, branching off from the well worn roads that all of us know so well.

I imagine that anyone who feels inspired to write and publish thoughts on the *mo'adim*, faces this struggle. He does not simply want to repeat what has already been said. If he were to do that, he could save himself the trouble of writing. On the other hand he knows that חדש אסור מן התורה and the last thing he wants to do is to pass on insights which, to borrow a phrase from the Chazon Ish in a critical assessment of a new book, אין בו ממה שנאמר למשה מסיני.

The solution of course lies in asking the right questions which, by definition, will always be new questions. It is to be expected that every generations sees things from its own unique perspective and that is as it should be. Again by definition, freshly minted questions will yield freshly minted answers. These will be new only in the sense that a polished diamond is new. Facets of the old are revealed which had always been there but which needed the deft hands of the polisher to make them really sparkle.

You have displayed the sure touch of the gifted craftsman. Your work has a lasting beauty which will give pleasure and inspiration to many generations of entranced readers.

We are all grateful to you. לך בכחך זה!

In friendship:

Moshe M. Eisemann

ERETZ YISROEL DURING THE MACCABEAN PERIOD

◆ ◆ ◆

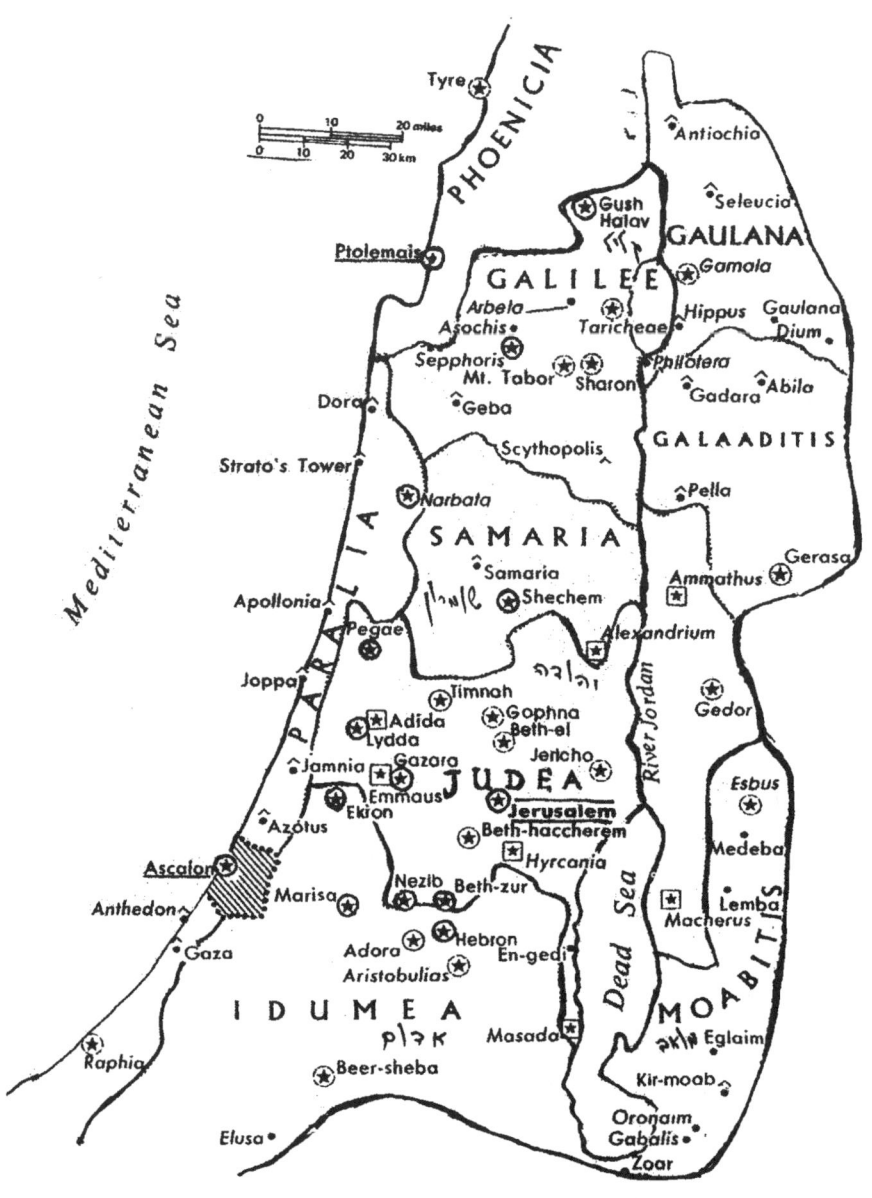

Acknowledgements and Thanks

This is the third volume of our effort to bring the depth, sophistication, drama and long term reverberations of Chanukah to the attention of readers. It is my hope that the uplifting inspiration of this volume will enhance your understanding and appreciation of this great epoch making event that assured the survival of *K'lal Yisrael*.

Special thanks to my editor, a brilliant and accomplished *talmid chochom*, writer and editor, the translator of the *ArtScroll Slichos*, Rabbi Yaakov Lavon, who has done so much to enhance this volume. Rabbi Lavon has brought the *Sifrei Chashmona'im* to life through his excellent editing.

Much appreciation to Yisroel Golding of Golding Designs who has produced the beautiful cover, to Moshe Kaufman of Israel Book Shop who has skillfully handled the distribution, to Henoch Levine of Tova Press for his professionalism and kindness, and to Ruthy Ungar for typing and retyping the manuscript with much skill.

I dedicate this volume to my wife Elaine whose patience and support made this volume possible. She personifies the nobility, *chessed* and dedication of the Jewish wife, mother, grandmother and great grandmother. May we be worthy to merit the growth and achievements in Torah and *yiras shomayim* of our children and grandchildren.

May the Torah learning inspired by this volume add to the *tefillos* of the *tzibur* for the *refuah sheleimah* of our daughter Malka Tovah Bas Chayah, may her husband Rabbi Dr. Chaim Kaweblum and their children enjoy Hashem's blessings for many years to come.

Songs and praises to the most Mighty and Kind, the *Ribono Shel Olam*, Who has given me the *z'chus* to witness His miracles, to dwell in the Tents of His Torah, and to be His agent in person and through my pen.

Kislev 5766/December 2006   Pinchas Stolper

Table of Contents

A Look at a Miracle 1
Introduction 3
The Birth of Idealistic Nationalism 6
Heroes and Puzzles 12
Why Did the Greeks Outlaw Mitzvos 16
Why Did the Greeks Stop Thinking? 24
The Challenge of Chanukkah 32

The Books of the Maccabees 39
The First Book of Maccabees 41
The Second Book of Maccabees 113

A Second Look 165
Books, Authors, and History 167
Chanukah Date Line 178
Chanukah Candle Lighting 180

A Look at a Miracle

Introduction

Looked at superficially, Chanukkah appears to be the simplest, least demanding of all of our festivals: its sum is candles, songs, prayers and (of course) traditional foods. But behind this seeming simplicity is a great depth of sophisticated meaning, an intricately resonating message that has sustained Israel through the ages. Under its surface, Chanukkah has a dramatic, almost romantic, poignancy; it is the 'do or die' story of the Jew confronting a hostile world.

This book is intended to introduce the only existing documents that fill out Chanukkah's history; accounts that purport to tell us what actually happened between the Jews and the Greeks. Admittedly, the two books of the Maccabees were not written with *ru'ach hakodesh*. They are strictly human accounts, and problematic ones at that, as explained in a special appendix to this book. All the same, these (and the works of Josephus) are the only ancient sources that exist, so we must extract the maximum benefit from them, however partial that may be. Maccabees I and II do certainly give us at least a taste of the background, history and spirit of these tragic and heroic days.

It is worthwhile finding out what the Maccabees faced and how their spirit rose to the occasion, because to this day Chanukkah challenges each Jew individually and the Jewish People collectively. The Chanukkah struggle was not a mere flash across the headlines, forgotten the next week. It was intended, in part, to prepare the Jewish Nation for the centuries of continuous exile that lay ahead. Wandering and persecution brought with them ideological challenges that are not unlike those our ancestors faced. Nor has anything changed today: our world continues to be preponderantly Greek in its culture.

Chazal taught, מַעֲשֵׂה אָבוֹת סִימָן לַבָּנִים, our ancestors' deeds map out the future course for their children. Chanukkah, then, is more than the celebration of a miraculous victory over a foe aiming at our destruction. The struggle with Greece reflects the challenges facing Jews still today in the United States, Europe and even Israel. Little has changed. In some countries Jews are challenged by the gentile upholders of Greek-derived culture; in others, loyal Jews confront Jewish secularists whose agenda is shockingly similar to that of the turncoat Jewish Hellenists. The lessons of the clash of Jews and Greeks are as relevant today as they were then.

For better or worse, the roots of Western culture go back to ancient Greece. Most contemporary Jews, then, live in a Greek-tinted world, think Greek-style thoughts, and pursue Greek values. In America it is no different, for while many of America's values are based on the Hebrew Scriptures, and while it is true that these values keep America civilized to an amazing degree, nonetheless much of the essence of American culture derives from the Greeks. Their ideals, their approach to life, and their view of its goals, all came to America through the Romans and their successors down the ages.

Ideals, values, goals: these are what define a civilization, for they are how it defines what is important and meaningful. Greece viewed man himself as "the measure of all things"*: it saw no higher goal than whatever man wanted, it equated "important" with "human desire," and defined "meaningful" as whatever man's frail intelligence could grasp. Nothing else was held to exist.

At the opposite pole is Jewish civilization, under which lies the realization that man is neither alone nor autonomous —that there exists a Supreme Power who holds each of us accountable. Jewish culture sees all meaning as coming from God, and finds meaning in life only insofar as each of us creates an intimate and significant relationship with his

---

* Plato, quoting Protagoras.

Creator—his Father—his ultimate Friend.

Between two such opposites, war was inevitable. As long as both opposites still exist, war is unending. But, as a people that abhors violence, we have carried on most of our war not with swords but with unique *mitzvos*. The better we understand these *mitzvos,* the more skilled warriors we become.

Authentic Jews need, therefore, to know what separates us from the secular values of Greek civilization. In other words, they need to understand the Chanukkah story. We must comprehend why so many Jews were drawn to Greek ways and why this attraction was—and is—inconsistent with the Torah's values. We must know why this attraction threatened the destruction of Jewish civilization: why the Maccabees went to war. Equally we need to know why and how they won, and what were the consequences of their victory.

The study of Chanukkah is the study of the conflict between Jews who maintained their loyalty to Torah, and Jews who submitted to Greek civilization in whole or in part, and thereby threatened Jewish life.

For those who, like us, live in what is called "the Western world," the Greeks and the Jews continue to represent the two basic world views that we meet every day. No nation proclaimed so rigorously as the Greeks a definition of life's purpose, meaning, and goals; no nation, that is, except the Jews. And the two definitions are poles apart. Our goal here is to understand what makes us Jews, and what still makes so much of the world Greek.

The Birth of Idealistic Nationalism

The Maccabees' decision to respond to oppression by military means was either an act of insanity or of heroic *Kiddush Hashem*. The Jews' situation was not just desperate, it was seemingly hopeless. They possessed few arms, no military experience or training, and no leadership. A significant part of the people had willingly become "Hellenizers," devotees of Greek culture; most of the rest had succumbed to the Hellenizers' demands out of fear for their lives. The remaining loyal Jews were few, frightened, isolated, and totally lacking popular support.

Under these circumstances the Maccabees began a war. Their fighting force began as a tiny, ragtag group of amateurs: to describe them as *yeshivah-bachurim* and householders would not be inaccurate. If one of its members were caught by either the Greeks or the Hellenizers, he would be killed instantly, just as would any Jew caught with a *sefer, tefillin, tallis* or *mezuzah*.

The Greek forces were numerous, fierce, well trained and equipped, vicious, and armed to the teeth. They had not only overwhelming number but overwhelming power on their side.

If so, the Jewish declaration of war was either an act of desperation or insanity, so unrealistic as to be laughable—unless Hashem might intervene to save His rebellious People. A military analyst would assume that the Maccabean fighters expected to die. Certainly they were prepared to do so. But they also believed that if they willingly sanctified His Name, God would protect them and ultimately grant them victory. In a way, we could agree with the military analyst and say that they had nothing to lose, for a life stripped of Torah was worthless to them. But more likely they thought they had everything to lose: everything that made life worthwhile. It is a matter of perspective.

All in all, we could say that the Maccabees were willing to fight for what they had to lose, and if they lost it they were willing to die. This defines their *Kiddush Hashem*.

They were not dreamers. They were idealists, and so would not abandon the Torah's way of life. But they were realists at the same time: they knew very well that the catastrophe they faced was decreed from Heaven, and that it was their fault.

It could not have happened, they knew, had God not decided that Israel's sins had reached the extreme limit. They had only to look at their own people to see mass abandonment of *mitzvos*, significant numbers of *Cohanim* involved in pagan practices, wanton depravity and immorality everywhere. At this rate there would soon be no Jewish People, and indeed the Greeks and their Jewish allies were committed to the ruthless elimination of Judaism. Once Judaism was gone the Jewish people would be gone too, for "we are only a nation because of the Torah."* Jewish nationalism is entirely idealistic, and now those ideals were in deadly danger.

Only one option remained: outright revolt, against both the Hellenizers and their Greek masters. Yet what could give such a hopeless war the chance of success? Paradoxically, the answer was their readiness to die, to offer their life for the sanctification of God's Name, to fight to the death even when there was no hope. It would be worthwhile if their sacrifice were acceptable to Heaven. If it was, maybe the Jewish loyalists could turn the tide. And at the least, they would die faithful to their Torah. There were no other options.

The Maccabees' battle cry—"Whoever is for Hashem, come to me!"—echoes a teaching of the Sages: when times are hard, *"We have no one to rely on—only Hashem."*** What

---

* R. Saadiah Gaon, *Emunos veDei'os*.

** Baraisa, end of Masseches Sotah.

Mattisyahu was saying was, "Is not Israel God's eternal people? Did we forget that a Jew's battles in this world are cosmic in scope? Did we forget that we are עַם עוֹלָם—an eternal people?" Martyrdom, then, was an intertwining of desperation, hope and resolute faith. Too many Jews had already died for no apparent purpose; the time had arrived for a new strategy. As the First Book of Maccabees reports,

> At that time in Yisrael, a group of lawless renegade Jews incited the people, telling them, 'Let us enter into a covenant with the surrounding Greeks, because disaster upon disaster has overtaken us since we segregated ourselves from them.' The people thought this a logical argument, and some of them in their enthusiasm even received authority from King Antiochus to introduce non-Jewish laws and customs. They built a sports stadium, a *gymnasion* in the Greek style, in Yerushalayim. They camouflaged the signs of their *bris milah* and repudiated the holy covenant of the Torah. They intermarried with Greeks and abandoned themselves to licentiousness and depravity.
>
> King Antiochus then issued a decree throughout his empire that all his subjects were to become one people and abandon their own laws and religion. The nations everywhere complied with the royal command, and many in Yisrael accepted Greek idolatry, sacrificing to idols and profaning the Shabbos. Moreover, the king sent agents with written orders to Yerushalayim and the towns of Judea, decreeing the introduction of Greek practices and customs foreign to the Jews. Burnt-offerings, sacrifices, and libations in the Temple were forbidden; *Shabbos* and *Yamim Tovim* were to be profaned; the Temple and its *Cohanim* and *Leviim* were to be rendered unclean. Altars, idols, and "sacred" precincts were to be established; swine and other un-

clean animals were to be offered in sacrifice. The Jews were forbidden to circumcise their sons; they were ordered to make themselves abominable, unclean, and profane in every way, and to abandon the Torah and change all their laws. The penalty for disobedience was death.

Such was the decree which the king issued to all his subjects. He appointed superintendents over all the people, and instructed each town of Judea to offer a sacrifice, town by town. People joined them in large numbers, every one of them a traitor to the Torah. Their wicked conduct throughout the land drove the observant Jews to hide in every possible place of refuge.

Pagan altars were built throughout the towns of Judea; incense was offered at the doors of houses and in the streets. All Torah scrolls that were found were torn apart and burned. Anyone discovered in possession of a Torah scroll, or conforming to the Torah, was put to death by the king's sentence.

The overseers offered sacrifices on the pagan altar, which was placed on top of the Temple altar. In accordance with the royal decree, they executed women who had had their children circumcised. Their babies, their families, and those who had circumcised them were hanged.... They welcomed death rather than defile themselves and profane the holy Torah's covenant, and so they died. The anger of Hashem was raging against Yisrael.

Mattisyahu replied... "Though all the nations of the king's dominions obey him and forsake their ancestral worship—though they have chosen to submit to his commands—yet I and my sons and brothers will follow the covenant of our fathers. Heaven forbid that we ever abandon the Torah and its statutes! We will not obey the king's command, nor will we deviate one step from the way of worship our tradition teaches."

"Many can easily be overpowered by a few—it makes no difference to Heaven; victory can be achieved by a few as easily as by many. Victory does not depend on numbers; strength comes from Heaven alone. Our enemies come filled with insolence and lawlessness to plunder and to kill us, our wives and children. But we are fighting for our lives and our Torah. Heaven will crush them before our eyes. You need not be afraid of them."

[The king] instructed Lysias to send a force to break and destroy the strength of Yisrael and those who were left in Yerushalayim, in order to blot out all memory of them from Yerushalayim and Judea.

"Better die fighting than look on while calamity overwhelms our people and the holy *Mikdash*. But it will be as Heaven wills."

"Do not be afraid of their great numbers, nor panic when they charge. Remember how our fathers were saved at the Red Sea, when Paroh and his army were pursuing them. Let us cry now to Heaven to favor our cause..."

Was this a war of martyrdom? Of suicide? Of self-delusion? It was certainly a war of *Kiddush Hashem,* and in such a war the answer to strategic problems was *teshuvah.* "We must return to our roots!" declared Mattisyahu, "and the Heavenly decree will be rescinded." That is just what happened: some Hellenizers repented, and the cowed masses of the people regained their courage. There was mass *teshuvah*. The Temple was cleansed. A small jar of sacred oil was found. The Menorah was relit. Imagine the people watching, first in dismay: *"Such a small jar,"*—*"only enough for one day"*—then in awe: *"it's still burning,"*—*"impossible,"*—*"it keeps burning."* People clamor to see the miracle. It keeps on burning for eight days. Light has been rekindled in the darkness, and the people whisper, *"Heaven has accepted our sacrifice."* And the lesson is learned: as long as "the Guardian of Israel neither sleeps nor slumbers," it does not matter how the gentile armies roar and rage.

Heroes and Puzzles

Chanukkah ranks among the greatest heroic stories of mankind, yet though it has been told and retold, most of the accounts are merely superficial. This is so partly because the Sages, our primary source, devoted only a few brief entries here and there to Chanukkah. Is it possible that the drama of those days was downplayed by the Sages? Is it possible that the tragedy was so embarrassing that they felt it should be minimalized? After all, the national crisis pointed to a major failure, an almost total breakdown of Jewish values. Indeed, how *could* a great people have fallen so low? Why do we hear of the initiative of Mattisyahu and his five sons, but of no one else? One doesn't know what to think; were there not other voices, other leaders?

Before they met the Greeks, the Jews had faced great pressure from formidable empires. They were continually enticed by the many cultures around them: Egypt, Aram, the Canaanites, the Babylonians, the Persians and the Medes. Each in turn tempted them to abandon their uniqueness; but the Jews did not succumb.

Israel's first serious ideological clash with a gentile culture was with the Greeks. And what made them so much more dangerous than the others? The fundamental difference was that they were a nation of philosophers. They did not merely indulge in vice, they justified it with (superficially) convincing arguments. Thus they presented Israel with an unprecedented—and unrelenting—ideological and intellectual challenge. At first the Greeks merely enticed; subsequently they demanded, on pain of death. But by the time they introduced force the war seemed mostly won. Many among Israel, including the rich and powerful, had succumbed to the smooth-talking Greek philosophers. Surely the masses would follow docilely?

They did not. Instead they followed the call of a tiny, neglected, "backwards," "superstitious" group—and defeated the Greek Empire. However, if we do not hear other voices or other leaders, it is most likely because there were none. The rich, the prominent, the "cream of society," had either sold themselves to the Greek pipe dream, or had quietly knuckled under to avoid trouble. Perhaps only Mattisyahu had the courage to protest, and perhaps only his sons at first had the courage to listen. In the end it did not matter, because Judaism has never gone according to majorities. Jews go according to the truth, even if only one man is brave enough to say it.

Chanukkah is the last festival of the Jewish historical calendar. It is the gateway to a two-thousand-year exile filled with wandering, persecution, expulsions, unexpected creativity and survival against all odds. The bloody trail of forced conversion and mass murder was laid by the world's most prominent and "civilized" nations. Yet, subsequent to the Chanukkah struggle, Jews met the most horrific persecution with steeled courage, heroism and martyrdom. That is the legacy of Chanukkah, and it is why no book was written for it.

The Sages did not record most of the story of Chanukkah in written form, because in its depths Chanukkah is the festival of the Oral—unwritten—Torah. In its most vital essence, "Torah" is not only that which is written in scrolls or books. It is not only the Mishnah, the Talmud, the many *midrashim* and mystical books. Torah is, most deeply of all, what is carried aloft in the minds and hearts of the great of Israel. Those minds and hearts are what won the Chanukkah war.

The Oral Torah is the sum total of the exposition of Torah found in the creative intellect of the great scholars of each generation. The oral nature of the Oral Torah is what keeps it fresh and vibrant, what makes it the central intellectual focus of both Israel's youth and Israel's sages. More than anything else, it is the soul and mind of the Jewish nation. And here is the central theme of Chanukkah: the Sages' iron determination that the Torah will remain inviolate, indestructible.

The paradox here is that the Sages of Israel, who best understood the lasting significance of the struggle with the Greeks, felt it best not to spell out some of the details for posterity. One might surmise that they were not anxious for later generations to become absorbed in the intricate study of the interplay of Greek and Jewish ideologies. Who are we, then, to go contrary to their wishes? But because the time we live in so significantly parallels the challenges of the Maccabean period, it is necessary, now as never before, to tell the story in depth. Today the Jewish people worldwide confront internal and external enemies that are very similar to the Hellenizers and the Greeks of old.

Yet, since the Sages initiated Chanukkah as a festival of the Oral Torah, necessarily they left it largely unwritten.* If we are to understand fully, we must search out every scrap of documentation available. Chiefly this consists of reading the traditional sources in the most subtle and alert ways possible, so as to grasp the full force of each statement. But even non-traditional sources, such as the ones presented in this book, have something to offer.

The Ramban writes,** "Were it not for the valiant efforts

---

* We must remember that during that entire era nothing was written down. Even the Talmud was not written down until the end of the period of the *Rabbanan Savoraei*, circa 560 C.E. Only Midrashim were transmitted in writing, based on the principle, "This is the time to act for Hashem."

** *Vayechi* 49:10.

of the Hasmoneans, Torah and *mitzvos* would have been obliterated from the Jewish Nation." What is more, without the determination, faith and courage of the High Priest Mattisyahu and his five valiant sons, the world—both Jewish and Western—would have come to a halt. Without the Oral Torah, and its stubbornly loyal adherents, there would have been little reason for, and little possibility of, the continued existence of the human race as we know it. To understand this one need only consider for a moment how likely it is that the world could have survived as a purely Greek world.

Despite the amazing revival of Torah in our days, the ideological battle of the Jewish Nation against Greece and Rome (*Eisav, Edom, Amalek*), Islamic culture (*Yishmael*), and the many assimilating Jews who are today's Hellenizers, is far from over.

Why Did the Greeks Outlaw Mitzvos?

The most basic thing to know about Chanukkah is that it was a response to oppression. In that case, a question needs to be asked first: Whatever possessed the Greeks, and the Jewish Hellenizers who collaborated with them, to attempt the destruction of Jewish life? Next we must ask, What spiritual failings left the Jews vulnerable to Hellenization? Once we have the answers to these questions, we will also understand why the Maccabean uprising brought about not only the defeat of Israel's enemies, but also a spectacular spiritual renaissance. To find our answers we can look first of all for Chanukkah's roots in the Torah.

Scripture often alludes to events that will take place in the future. Some of its predictions are clearly stated, while some are cryptic references that were deciphered for us by our Sages. Among these is a reference to the wars of the Maccabees, in the blessing Moshe Rabbenu gave to the tribe of Levi before his death. The verse can be translated, "Hashem will bless [Levi's] army and favor the work of his hands. He will strike down his opponents, and smite his enemies beyond rising again."[*]

And what does this have to do with Chanukkah? Everything, when one remembers that the Maccabees were descendants of Levi. Rashi explains that Moshe Rabbenu, when he gave his blessing, saw that "one day in the future the *Chashmonai* [*i.e.* Mattisyahu, who was descended from the priestly House of Chashmon] and his sons would wage war against the Greeks. Moshe therefore prayed for a Divine blessing upon them, because they were so few... against

---

[*] Deuteronomy 33:11.

myriads of Greeks."[*]

The entire Maccabean fighting force was originally the twelve descendants of Chashmon and their confederate Elazar. Thirteen men against the Hellenic Empire! And most of their own nation had deserted the cause. Even after the rebels' ranks began to swell, they were still a bare handful, mostly of them *Cohanim* and *Leviim*—men utterly unaccustomed to warfare. At its greatest strength the Maccabean "army" was like a pebble going up against a boulder, and most of its members were better at *davening* than at swordplay. (It has been said jokingly that the greatest miracle of Chanukkah was that the Maccabees did not accidentally cut their own fingers off with their swords.) However, they were indeed experts at praying, and they used this advantage against the Greeks to the fullest. And it won them the war.

Moshe Rabbenu, too, seeing this "impossible" situation looming centuries in the future, took a totally practical approach: he asked Divine blessing for the outnumbered, inept fighters. "God will bless [Levi's] army and favor the work of his hands." (Implicit in Rashi's statement is that these Jews' willingness to make what was, to most people's mind, a hopeless effort, was in itself miraculous, and therefore deserved blessing.) Once this "secret weapon" was unleashed, the Greeks had not a chance of success. It all comes down to how one views "practicality."

Perhaps the reason why the Greeks could not bear to see Jews keeping *mitzvos* was just this kind of clash in views. For alone among ancient cultures, Greece was a nation of philosophers. In addition, Greece was arguably the most arrogant of all nations. By consequence they insisted on their opinions being accepted by all as absolute and final. For example, if Greeks think that material ways and means

---

[*] Rashi *ad loc.*

are the only practical ones, and prayer and faith are mere delusions, then everyone must agree. If Greeks consider man to be a creature of body and mind but no more, then a nation that adds a soul to the equation—and even dares to proclaim the soul most important!—must be beaten down and forced to abandon its crazed idea. If Greeks live for pleasure, all their subjects must do the same, and a people that lives according to ethical principles is an unbearable insult.

Greece was the first society in history in which worship was not a part of daily life. Epicurus had long ago laid down the rule that the gods never trouble themselves with the affairs of the world; and Plato went one step farther and declared that the gods never did anything at all!* While Israel based reality on spirituality, Greece believed only in material things. Greece was self-centered; Israel was God-centered.

None of these contrasts were significant—until the reign of Antiochos Epiphanes. Until then the Greeks had only conquered peoples who, by and large, saw things the same way as themselves: people whose native cultures preached egotism and a life based on gratification. They had simply not noticed a tiny people tucked away in a corridor of their empire, who thought very differently indeed.

They might never have noticed, but for a group of "enlightened, progressive" Jews and their petition to the government. They asked legal backing for their campaign to bring their "backward" brethren into line with modern civilization. And when the Greeks heard the details of this small nation's beliefs and practices, they were outraged at this "*apikorsus*" and organized a major operation, both administrative and

---

* His reason is horrifyingly Greek: since, he said, no one ever acts unless to gratify a desire, and since the gods, being perfect, already have everything they could desire, therefore they would never stir themselves to do anything. It seems that Greek "gods," like Greek people, were only interested in getting pleasure for themselves.

military, to force the "sinners" into compliance with Greek doctrine.

The next question is, what was the war's spiritual root? In other words, what was the Jews' sin? Why did God allow the Greeks to proceed with their hateful plans? R. Yoel Sirkis[*] teaches that it was the result of הִתְרַשְּׁלוּת בָּעֲבוֹדָה, a perfunctory, sloppy approach to the Temple service that had become widespread among the *Cohanim*. This would, of course, have led to a similar lack of devotion to *mitzvos* among the general populace.

The theme of neglect of the commandments and inevitable Heavenly retribution is found many times over in the *Chumash* and the books of the Prophets. Taking the Torah for granted, togther with a lack of zeal in worship and observance, have often been the cause of Israel's crises. In this case the result was a military confrontation with the Greeks, but the root cause was spiritual.

How did the Greeks come to exert such a strong influence on the Jewish people? Actually, the Greek influence on the peoples of the ancient world was profound. Greek had long become the chief language of educated people in the entire Mediterranean Basin, and then, with Alexander, it had spread throughout the Near East. Its dominance was such that, 150 years before the Chanukkah confrontation,[**] the Greek king of Egypt,[***] Ptolemy II, compelled the seventy members of the Sanhedrin to translate the Torah into Greek,

---

[*] "The *Bach*," author of the *Bayis Chadash* on the *Tur* and notes on the Gemara.

[**] In approximately 285 BCE.

[***] After the death of Alexander the Great, his generals divided up his empire among themselves. The House of Ptolemy took the land from Egypt to the Syrian border, including Eretz Yisrael, until later the House of Seleucus added Eretz Yisrael to its Syrian domains.

creating a work called the Septuagint. We must note that each member of the Sanhedrin was so fluent in Greek that he could translate the text of the entire Torah!

With a nation's language come its world of ideas and its culture. Not only the Sages, but the Jewish *intelligentsia* of the time was proficient in the Greek language—and therefore had learned to think somewhat in Greek terms and had studied the works of the Greek philosophers. From the time of Alexander's conquest of the ancient world, Jews began to develop a measure of comfort with the Greek lifestyle that was much more damaging than the American Jews' involvement in American civilization today, because, besides hedonism and materialism, it involved a strong pagan element.

As Greek civilization aggressively attempted to foist itself on the Jews, it weakened the morale, loyalty and resolve of large numbers among them. The Greek influence was so compelling that not only did it seduce some Jews away from observance, it corrupted the inner hearts even of those who remained outwardly loyal to the Torah. Eventually significant numbers of Jews, among them many *Cohanim*, no longer looked at the Temple and its service with the passion and weightiness they demanded. Because of this, the Greeks and their Jewish "fellow travelers" were at last able to order the termination of the Temple service.* Hashem dealt with His people measure for measure: had they revered the Temple service properly, no one could ever have stopped them from keeping it. Once they ceased caring about it, the Greeks could move in. As it were, they now had permission from Heaven.

Antiochus was told by his assimilated Jewish advisors about a particular mitzvah that inspired the Jews: the daily

---

* In fact, a *Baraisa* (a Rabbinic teaching from the time of the Mishnah) records that stopping the daily *Tamid* sacrifice was the first anti-Jewish decree from the Greeks.

lighting of the Temple Menorah. So long as the Jews kindled this flame, they felt that they were invincible and eternal. In order to stamp out this feeling, the Greeks were careful to defile all of the Temple's store of pure oil in their attempt to remove the last remaining source of Jewish inspiration.

That the Hellenizers were right about the Menorah is evidenced by the institution of Chanukkah lamps. The desecration of the pure oil and the miracle of the only remaining flask, enough for one day, reflect the underlying issues of Chanukkah. Like the Menorah and its oil, the spirit of the Jewish People had been defiled by the Greeks. Only a remaining handful possessed the will to wage battle for God and His Torah. Few even believed that resistance was possible—perhaps only for a brief battle, but no more. Yet suddenly the Jewish People's will was resurrected, and the handful of visionaries brought forth renewed light, not only for a day but for generations to come.

There is no explaining the war that followed according to military rules. Strategically it was lost before it began; but when significant numbers of Jews displayed readiness to sacrifice their lives to protect the Temple and uphold its service, God blessed them with a series of miraculous victories. As the war progressed, many Hellenized Jews began to realize their errors and mended their ways, leading to still more victories against ever-growing armies of Greeks.

This is the reason the crowning miracle of Chanukkah, the Menorah, took place in the Temple, and only *after* the Temple was recaptured and cleansed by the Maccabees. It was a Heavenly salute to the self-sacrificing idealism of the Maccabees, and a last acknowledgement that the hand of God had been in the miraculous revival of Jewish life.

Many Jews today celebrate Chanukkah without having any clear idea of its meaning. Each branch of the divided Jewish People has injected its own ideology into Chanukkah, turning it into a holiday of lights, or of belligerent nationalism, or of freedom of conscience. None of these "rewrites" is a good fit.

It does not help matters that our principal sources of information are two non-Biblical, purely historical works: the books of Maccabees and the writings of Josephus Flavius. These books go into some detail about the religious, political and military aspects of Chanukkah, but lack depth. They do not even begin to fathom the spiritual and ideological bedrock of the Maccabean revolt; that is, they do not benefit from our Sages' understanding of Chanukkah's meaning. Only they revealed the inner message of the festival, and for this they used but few words. The lack of meaningful source material is doubtless one cause of the trivialization of Chaukkah.

Yet today more than ever a deep understanding of Chanukkah is needed. For our own time is in many ways similar to the era of the Maccabees. Today most Jews are Westernizers, like the Hellenizers of those days. Many Jews even behave like the Hellenizers, in active opposition to authentic Judaism. Once again Torah Jewry are the few against the many. Those who value what is holy are once again battling those who would "reform" the Torah's way of life.

It was pointed out by R. Mattisyahu Salomon, the *Mashgiach* of Beth Medrash Govoha of Lakewood, that today too many observant Jews are guilty of הִתְרַשְּׁלוּת בָּעֲבוֹדָה, neglect of the Divine Service. How? A significant portion of our daily prayers is the *Korbanos*, speaking of the Temple Service as it once was. Because the daily *Shacharis* is often rushed, it has become a common practice to skip this portion of the service. However, this recitation fills in the gap left in our souls by the missing Temple Service, and it is a strong force in bringing about the restoration of the *Beis Hamikdash* and its Service, speedily, in our day.

R. Salomon's admonition is something we should all take seriously. Just a few additional minutes are enough to say at least a portion of the Temple Service, sending a powerful message. May it be Hashem's will that He restore our ancient glories.

Why Did the Greeks Stop Thinking?

My first trip to the Acropolis of Athens was during the summer of 1999, when my wife and I toured Greece and saw the remnants of the ancient Greek civilization at first hand. This famous group of buildings provided a deeper appreciation of the grandeur and power of the only other civilization which did what the ancient Jews did: to think—to seek answers for man's quest for truth and purpose.

Among the ancients, only the Greeks and the Jews attempted to answer life's ultimate questions. The Jews succeeded in their quest. The Greeks created not only schools of philosophy but a grand civilization—whose economic base was mass slavery. Looked at from a twentieth-century perspective, Athenian democracy was not a democracy at all. Only the male aristocracy, 10% of the population, were enfranchised. The balance—foreigners, women, slaves, the landless—had few or no rights. Yet Greek democracy was a cut above the autocratic monarchies that were its contemporaries.

The Jewish confrontation with Greece (and its successor empire, Rome) was caused by the Greeks' repeated effort to subdue the Jews, primarily by attempting to force them to abandon their faith, philosophy and way of life. The Greeks vehemently rejected the Jewish concepts of God, faith, morality and ethics. They specifically could not tolerate the Jewish idea of chosenness and the intimate relationship the Jews claimed to have with God.

But the Greeks saw that persuasion would not succeed, so they chose force in their attempt to obliterate Jewish civilization, imposing the death penalty on any Jew who would teach or observe his religion. The Chanukkah victory marks Judaism's successful confrontation with Greek ideology, and with its temporal power.

Ages later, the result is that ancient Greece and Rome no longer exist. Despite nostalgic pretenses, today's inhabitants of Rome and Greece have very little connection with their forebears. Nor do they retain, or even relate to, their ancient culture and heritage. Their connection with ancient times was severed by the conquest of their lands by barbarian hordes, other cultures and empires, as well as by their adoption of Christianity. We find the ancient Greeks and Romans today only in the dust of ancient buildings and statues, in literature, art and in history books. Their civilization is long dead, and the great thinkers, Socrates, Plato and Aristotle, Sophocles and Euripides, have lost their attraction for modern thinkers. Judaism, however, has survived, and offers as much to the world today as it ever did.

In a deeper and more ultimate sense, Greece and Rome were actually defeated by the Jews. This happened when these pagan peoples totally abandoned their pagan beliefs, thought system, mythology, philosophy and social structure, and instead accepted a world view based on that of the Jews. Today's Greeks and Romans are descendants of people who converted to Christianity in the easrly centuries of the Common Era and, in so doing, accepted some major principles of the Jewish Bible as the new basis for their lives. Notions of human equality, Sabbath rest, the significance of family, of one all-powerful God, and an afterlife; today's accepted views of morality, salvation, messiah, creation and much more; all were Jewish "innovations" that the Greeks and Romans had attempted to obliterate, yet later accepted docilely.

The differences between Judaism and Christianity are fundamental, broad, and deep, yet Christianity represents the attempt of a deviant Jewish sect to disseminate and impose their form of Judaism on the world—an altered, even a distorted form, yet a form of Judaism, still preserving much of its core beliefs. By accepting the Bible, the Greeks acquiesced in a revolutionary change in their way of life and worship. We can say that centuries later the Chanukkah war was still being fought, and that the Greeks had just lost another battle.

During my brief visit to their country, I asked a number of intelligent and educated Greeks the following questions:

Why did the Greeks adopt the Jewish world view (at least partly) after so fiercely opposing it?

What happened to the intellectual impulses that had fired the Greek search for truth?

Why didn't the era of the great Greek philosophers continue through the ages as it did for the Jews, for whom thought has always been at the core of their lives?

Why didn't the Greek adoption of the Bible lead to a further study of Judaism and a refinement of their religious faith?

These questions are the more pointed when we compare Hellenism to other cultures. The Egyptian, Babylonian, Phoenician, Mesopotamian, and Persian religious systems were "copycat" pagan systems, all much the same, which revered and searched for the Divine but did not have a clue where to find it. These nations left no meaningful religious literature, indicating the absence of a serious attempt to deal with life's basic issues. In contrast, the ancient Greeks, most especially the Athenians, created a literature and a thought system that demonstrated a serious search for truth. Why did this search stop at Christian dogma and not seek deeper truths?

The puzzle is even deeper: for if the Greeks were convinced that their paganism, all the societal, philosophical and religious approaches with which they had experimented, failed to offer satisfactory answers, why did they accept Christianity, which was, at best, only a superficial and diluted form of Judaism? Furthermore, the Greek populace did not study the Bible, its thought system, and the *mitzvos* that were retained in Christianity, with anything like the depth, seriousness, and scholarship with which they created their own thought system at the height of their culture. Quite the opposite: they infused their local version of Christianity with much of their discarded pagan thought and practices, and numerous vestiges of their abandoned culture. Several of their pagan gods were even conveniently turned into Christian saints.

One would expect a nation which had developed a unique form of intellectualism, that at one time pervaded the entire known world, to try to continue that intellectual tradition. Why didn't the Greeks utilize their intellectual powers and follow their initial acceptance of partial Judaism to its logical conclusion? Why did they not adopt the pure monotheism of Judaism together with its all-encompassing system of literature, thought and mitzvah practice?

We know that many individual Greeks and Romans did, in fact, do so. According to some sources, including Josephus, thousands of Romans, including prominent members of the aristocracy and the Roman Senate, converted to Judaism. But they did not create a lasting indigenous movement.

Finally, why is there no contemporary attempt to confront this mystery? Why does a major portion of the civilized world practice religions that drew their power and strength from Judaism—that attempted in some limited form to emulate the Jewish life they met in Palestine and the Diaspora—and that stopped before any serious, in-depth study of the Jewish viewpoint? It is estimated that following the *Churban*, the destruction of the Holy Temple and the Jewish state, Jews constituted ten per cent of the population of the Mediterranean basin. Why did so few Greeks and Romans have the intellectual honesty to fully examine the root source and foundation of their newly-adopted lifestyle?

Interestingly, the modern Greeks with whom I spoke acknowledged that my questions were valid. They even pressed me to propose answers. I could only reply, "Follow the example of your ancestors, Sophocles, Plato and Aristotle, and search for your own answers. Ask yourselves: Why are the Jews an eternal people who, despite the attempts of the Greeks, Romans, Persians, Egyptians, Babylonians, Assyrians, and others to destroy them, remain a dynamic force in the world today? Why is Greece today a backward country with little to show for its former grandeur? Finally, why aren't these questions posed? Why is there so little search for truth?"

Today's Greece truly is a pathetic shadow of ancient Greece. It is a drab, colorless, country that lacks political power, industry, technology, creative thinkers, religious and secular leaders. Its ancient writings have created no living heritage. All that remains is the memory of the past. No one has taken the place of the old philosophers; no one attempts to complete the task they initiated.

What Christianity provided the Greeks was a half-baked, semi-pagan, semi-monotheistic system that accompanied Europe through its Dark Ages. For generations, thought, inquiry, literacy, education, philosophy, technology and science were monitored and even suppressed. The quest for truth was put down by intimidation, until almost all voices of creative intellectualism were stilled.

Two millenia later, the West has now come to a philosophical and theological dead end. It has, however, accomplished two things. First, it has abandoned the iron vise of paganism, hitching its wagon instead to a weak derivative of Judaic monotheism. Second, it has co-opted the Bible as its wellspring of inspiration and values. Yet it has consistently ignored Judaism's tradition of deep wisdom. It has neglected the Bible's original Hebrew text, which alone is comprehensible, unlike all the many "translations." It has ignored the exegesis of the Midrash which converts the Bible from an enigmatic text to a refreshing source of meaningful answers and truths. Unable to face the inconsistencies of Christian scriptures and the horrific record of churchly corruption, prejudice, inhumanity, hatred, narrowness, and anti-Semitism, western civilization, for all its achievements, refuses to think through its adoption of monotheism to a logical conclusion.

It is not surprising, then, that Western Europe's largest churches are shockingly abandoned these days, reduced to monuments for the admiration of tourists. There is good reason for this neglect. In a recent book, *The Cube and the Cathedral,* George Weigel describes Europe as a culture that has become not only increasingly secular, but downright hostile to its own Christian roots. "European man has convinced himself that in order to be modern and free, he must be radically secular," Mr. Weigel writes. "That conviction and its public consequences are at the root of Europe's contemporary crisis of civilizational morale.

"Christianity is considered retrograde and atavistic in a 'progressive' society devoted to the good life, long holidays, short work hours and generous government benefits."

According to this new European philosophy, concepts such as "justice" or "freedom," and qualities such as "evil" or "good," do not exist in the abstract but are merely words, denoting a single instance of what they describe. They are not universal concepts, just words good enough to describe today. A current of thought has been set into motion that has pulled European man away from transcendent truths. A major casualty of this new philosophy is the idea of human nature: it is supposed nowadays not to exist.

"If there is no such thing as human nature," Mr. Weigel argues, "then there are no universal moral principles that can be read from human nature." If there are no universal moral truths, then religion, which posits them, is merely an oppressive myth, from which Europe's elite see themselves as liberated.

"The issue ultimately involved," continues Mr. Weigel, "is whether there is a course of truth higher than, and independent of man, and the answer to the question is decisive for one's view of the nature and destiny of humankind."

In what is certainly the most attention-grabbing passage in the book, Mr. Weigel sketches the worst-case scenario— the "bitter end"—for a Europe that is religiously bereft, demographically moribund and morally without a compass: "The muezzin summons the faithful to Moslem prayer from the central mosque of St. Peter's in Rome, while Notre-Dame has been transformed into Hagia Sophia on the Seine—a great Christian church that has become an Islamic museum."

Without a religious dimension, Mr. Weigel argues, commitment to human freedom is likely to be too weak for people to be willing to make sacrifices in its name. We can already see how Europe's political elite are reluctant to put "the good life" on hold and put lives on the line when freedom is in need of a champion—say in the Balkans, or especially in Iraq.

The good of freedom for European citizens must nowadays be weighed against the cost of actually fighting for it; freedom is no longer an absolute, transcendent value. In such a world as this, governed by a narrow utilitarian calculus, sacrifice is rare, and churches go unvisited. It is reminiscent of when the Greeks abandoned their gods and stopped thinking. This spelled the end of Greek civilization, and it would seem to spell the end of European civilization in our day.[*]

Is it possible that thinking Catholics are still in shock over the role Catholic countries played in the Holocaust? They might (we hope) be especially ashamed of the apa-

---

[*] Not that European Christianity is blameless for its rejection by Europeans, but that is a topic for a different book.

thetic, almost collaborationist conduct of Pope Pius XI and his successor Pius XII. Or perhaps it is the fifteen centuries of oppression, the mass expulsions, the Crusades, corruption, immoral behavior, *autos da fé*? Is killing innocents religion? Unfortunately Catholicism plays a dual, indeed a schizophrenic role in most people's lives, as recent events have made painfully obvious.

The larger question is, are the Europeans now committing the intellectual and spiritual suicide that the ancient Greeks did?

We know that one day the truths of Judaism in their pure form will be understood and accepted by the world at large. For the moment, Jewish scholars debate whether the introduction of Christianity to the world was a step toward or away from that goal. All the same, though, some originally Jewish concepts have been adopted by the nations in place of totally pagan ideas.

Perhaps, too, the world will start thinking again. Perhaps it will take outright miracles to begin that process; but whatever the case, our task is clear. The Jewish People must continue to set a moral, ethical, intellectual and spiritual example that cannot be ignored or denied by anyone. In that way the pure truth of Torah will be recognized when the right time arrives.

The Challenge of Chanukkah

What is the essence of the human being? What makes us unique creatures? What is the core of our *tzelem Elokim*, our having been created in the image of God? Surely it should be in discovering our true hopes, dreams, ideals and goals. But even if we are clear as to what these are, how important are they to us? To what degree do they motivate our actions and determine our thoughts? What are we prepared to sacrifice in order to protect the ideals we value most?

What dominates our lives? Our pursuit of money, power and possessions, or our quest as a Torah Jew to forge an intimate relationship with God?

Suppose I asked you, "Given the world as we know it, given the enemies that surround us, given the dangers that face our people—what are the dreams that fill your heart on Chanukkah?" Wouldn't you agree that they are all about yearning for the miracles God did for our fathers, the Maccabees? Aren't you dreaming and wishing that they would happen in our day, at this time, בַּזְּמַן הַזֶּה?

As a child in 1939, I watched my father cry as he sat at his radio and heard news of the early stages of the Holocaust. It was then that I developed the habit of standing in front of the Chanukkah menorah, staring at its tiny lights, trying to comprehend their message. I remember saying over and over again, "Hashem, please do it again. We need Your miracles today, as much as the Maccabees did two thousand years ago."

The *Al Hanissim* prayer indicates that the primary miracle of Chanukkah was the military victory, and makes it clear that the victory was possible only because of God's miraculous intervention. This gives rise to three questions:

Why do we celebrate a great military victory with tiny,

fragile flames? Surely there should be a symbolism more in consonance with the nature of the miracle.

Since the primary miracle was the military one, why did the Sages choose to institute an observance—the Chanukkah menorah—which commemorates a secondary miracle which took place after the victory?

What was God's message to the Jewish People when oil sufficient for one night glowed for eight? No miracle is without a message. Indeed, this is the miracle that we commemorate in tangible form for eight nights. Surely it represents the essence of Chanukkah.

The answer to all three questions lies in understanding the nature of fire. Flame is a physical manifestation of the spiritual: נֵר ה' נִשְׁמַת אָדָם —"God's candle is the soul of man." Like the human spirit, a flame can die or soar; it can be extinguished easily or it can light up the entire world. All one need do is provide sufficient fuel.

The essence of the Jew is his spirit, his inner flame. The menorah of Chanukkah commemorates the steadfast resilience, the self-sacrifice of the Jewish spirit, the stubbornness of a "stiff-necked people" in the face of fierce opposition, persecution and overwhelming military might.

The miracle of the oil was a reflection of the underlying miracle of Chanukkah: the resurrection of the will of the Jewish People to resist the Greeks. Just as the Holy Temple's oil had been defiled by the Greeks, the spirit of the Jewish People also had been defiled by them. Almost no one remained who possessed the will to wage the battle for God and His Torah. Scores of thousands of Judean families had been Hellenized or intimidated into accepting the decrees of the Greeks forbidding the study of Torah and the observance of *mitzvos*. The light of the Jewish People was all but extinguished.

In the midst of this hopeless situation there arose a family of priests, Mattisyahu and his five sons, who advocated armed rebellion. The family of Mattisyahu was the only pure, undefiled flask of holy oil remaining among the Jewish People. As the oil could not last for eight days, so there was no way that a group of untrained young people could even threaten, still less subdue, the greatest military machine ever created up to that time. And not only were the Maccabees battling the Greeks but also their fellow Jews who had caved in and adopted the Greek way of life.

Before they could successfully unfurl the banner of revolt, the Maccabees (the sons of Mattisyahu and their tiny army) had to revive the spirit of the Jewish People. They had to reawaken the Jew's faith in God so He would become their ally. In the *Al Hanissim* prayer we read: "רַבְתָּ אֶת רִיבָם, You fought their fight." Once we were prepared to go to war on God's behalf, once it became our battle, only then did it become God's battle, so that He fought on our behalf.

In the end, that one untainted family succeeded in rekindling the pure flame of Torah, which in turn revived the spirit of the Jewish nation and its determination to resist its enemies for all time. It is this victory, the victory of the Jewish spirit and intellect, of indomitable faith and determination, which we celebrate with the kindling of the Chanukkah menorah. It is this spiritual obstinacy, the call for all-out resistance, that God acknowledged with the miracle of the flask of oil. The war was miraculous, the victories defied logic; but to cynics, victories are bravery, luck, determination, and creative strategy. How was the generation to know that the victories were truly miraculous? Only a miracle which left no doubt would assure even the cynics.

The miracle of Chanukkah repeats itself in each generation, both "in those days" and also "at this time." The revival of Torah in our day is no less a miracle; the odds are no less formidable; the faith and determination required are no less.

The forces of Western civilization—which place material goods, secular "values," and technology above the Torah's values—are Greek philosophy in modern dress. Today's adoption, by the majority of Jews, of secular values and immoral lifestyles mimics the Hellenization of Jewish society in ancient times. Secular philosophy, which denies the uniqueness and supremacy of Torah and the reality of God's Will, remains our greatest enemy.

When we sing the Chanukkah hymn, *Ma'oz Tzur*, we should pause over its poignant stanza "יְוָנִים נִקְבְּצוּ עָלַי, Greeks have overwhelmed me." That is just the plight of the majority of Jews today: they are overwhelmed by the secular, mechanized life around them. But if we succeed in rekindling the light of authentic Judaism, we can replicate the miracle of Chanukkah.

Let us not mince words. Something ominous, even frightful, is enveloping all of *Klal Yisrael*, the Jewish People. A massive spiritual decline has overtaken most of the world Jewish community. Recent sociological studies indicate that in ten years the majority of American Jews will no longer be Jewish. A million and a half American Jewish children are not receiving a meaningful Jewish education. The intermarriage rate is well over fifty per cent. A million Jewish children in Israel cannot tell you the meaning of *Sh'ma Yisrael*. They are alienated from their Jewish heritage, despite the fact that they live in what is supposed to be a Jewish state.

There is one difference, though, between today and ancient times. This is that, for the first time, many secular Jews also realize their peril. They are beginning to acknowledge that they are unable to insure their own Jewish survival without calling upon the ideals and practices of Torah Jewry.

There is another side to the coin. The accomplishments of the American and Israeli *Teshuvah* (return-to-Judaism) movements—in terms of their impact on people's lives and on Jewish communities—is unprecedented. Suddenly, during the 1960s and '70s, a new and unexpected voice was heard. It was the voice of youth speaking out on behalf of *kedu-*

shah and mitzvah observance. Yeshivos and women's seminaries, catering to the needs of Jews searching for their spiritual roots, became fixtures in the Jewish world. Teshuvah programs for youth and adults were established. It was found that when Jews experience the warmth and truth of Torah, they are attracted to Judaism despite the competition of an earthy popular culture.

Our Maccabean ancestors call to us from their graves: "Repeat the miracle of Chanukkah for yourselves! As it was 'in those days,' let it be so 'in our time.'" The question is, who among us will respond to their call?

The sixth chapter of Exodus states that God answered the cries of the Jews enslaved in Egypt, saying, "I also have heard the cry of the Jewish people." The Chasam Sofer asks, "What is the meaning of 'and *I also* have heard'? Who else would have heard but God?" He explains that a transformation had taken place among the Jews. They began caring about each other and performing acts of kindness for one another. Jews began hearing each other's cries and began praying for each other and for the entire Jewish People. Most important of all, they stopped speaking *lashon hara*, harmful speech aimed against each other. A new camaraderie took hold and unity emerged. Only then did God respond to their prayers. Only when they heard *each other's* pleas and responded to them did God come to their assistance, saying, "*I, too, have heard their cries.*"

The Gemara asks simply, "What is the essence of Chanukkah?" Its reply is "דְּלָא לְמִסְפַּד בְּהוֹן, It is forbidden to mourn [or be depressed] during Chanukkah." The Maccabean victory grew out of the fact that the Jewish People discovered its inner strength to overcome despair and fight against unbelievable odds. Can we, in our day, unfurl the banner of the Maccabees? Can we call out to our fellow Jews, "מִי לַה' אֵלַי—Whoever believes in our cause, join us"?

The Maccabees reversed the Hellenizing tide of their generation and brought about miracles. We can, and must, do as much.

The Books of The Maccabees

THE FIRST BOOK OF THE MACCABEES

Chapter 1:
Antiochus and the Jewish revolt

Philip's son Alexander was a Macedonian and the king of Greece. He marched from Greece, defeated Darius, king of Persia and Media, and seized his throne. Following this spectacular victory, he waged many campaigns in the far corners of the earth, capturing fortified towns, slaughtering kings, and plundering innumerable nations. When at last the world was subdued under his rule and acknowledged his sovereignty, his pride knew no limits; he built up a titanic army and ruled over countries, nations, and dominions, all of which paid him tribute.

When he fell ill and knew he was dying, he summoned his generals and nobles who had been his childhood friends, and divided his empire among them while he was still alive. Alexander had reigned twelve years when he died. His generals took over the government, each in his own province. On his death they were all crowned kings, and their descendants succeeded them for many years. Despotic rulers, they brought untold miseries upon the world.

A scion of this stock was the wicked Antiochus Epiphanes, son of King Antiochus. The Romans held him hostage in Rome before he succeeded to the Greek throne [of the province of Syria] in the year 137 of the Greek era [175 BCE].

At the same time in Yisrael, a group of lawless renegade Jews incited the people, telling them, 'Let us enter into a covenant with the surrounding Greeks, because disaster upon disaster has overtaken us since we segregated ourselves from them.' The people thought this a logical argument, and some of them, in their enthusiasm, even received authority from King Antiochus to introduce non-Jewish laws and customs. They built a sports stadium, a *gymnasion* in the Greek style, in Yerushalayim. They camouflaged the signs of their *bris milah* and repudiated the holy covenant of the Torah. They intermarried with Greeks and abandoned themselves to licentiousness and depravity.

When he was firmly established on his throne, Antiochus was determined to become king of Egypt and to rule over both Egypt and Syria. He assembled a powerful force of chariots, elephants, cavalry, and a great fleet, and invaded Egypt. In the heat of the battle, Ptolemy king of Egypt panicked and fled, abandoning his troops, many of whom were already dead. Antiochus then captured and pillaged the fortified towns, establishing his sovereignty.

While returning from the conquest of Egypt, in the year 143, Antiochus led his forces against Yisrael and Yerushalayim. In his arrogance he entered the Temple and carried off the golden altar, the *Menorah* with all its utensils, the *Shulchan* for the *Lechem HaPanim*, the sacred cups and bowls,

---

renegade Jews: the Hellenizers

gymnasion: a Greek word meaning "place where people exercise naked."

the year 143: 169 BCE

the shulchan for the Lechem HaPanim: the golden table with the "show-bread" displayed upon it the golden censers, the *Paroches* before the *Kodesh kodashim,* and the crowns. He stripped all the gold plating from the Temple façade and seized the silver, gold, precious vessels, and whatever secret treasures he found, taking them all with him when he left for his own country. Arrogantly he gloated over the resulting bloodshed and the utter desecration of the Temple.

> Great was our lamentation throughout Yisrael!
> Rulers and elders groaned in bitter grief.
> Maidens and young men were despondent;
> Our beautiful women were disfigured.
> Every bridegroom took up the lament,
> And every bride sat grieving in her chamber.
> The land trembled for its inhabitants,
> And all the House of Yaakov was overcome with
>   shame.

Two years later, King Antiochus sent a senior officer of the royal revenues to the towns of Judea. He arrived at Yerushalayim with a strong force of soldiers: his language was friendly, but deceptively so. As soon as he gained the city's confidence, he suddenly attacked, inflicting many casualties, plundering the city, and setting it ablaze. He destroyed houses and walls on every side, imprisoned women and children, and seized the cattle.

The City of David was turned into a citadel, inclosed by a high, thick wall with strong towers, and was garrisoned by impious Greek sinners—Syrian foreigners—and Jewish

---

censers: used for offering the incense

paroches: the embroidered curtain that veiled the holiest parts of the *Mikdash*

Kodesh kodashim: the "holy of holies," where the Ark of the Covenant was kept

renegades. Having made themselves secure within the citadel, they accumulated arms and provisions, and deposited all they had plundered from Yerushalayim. There they lay in ambush, a lurking threat to the Temple and a constant menace to Yisrael.

> They shed the blood of innocents,
> they defiled the *Beis HaMikdash*.
> The citizens of Yerushalayim fled in fear.
> Yerushalayim became the abode of aliens,
> a stranger to her own offspring:
> her children deserted her.
> Her *Mikdash* lay desolate as a wilderness;
> her holidays were turned to mourning,
> her *Shabbasos* to a reproach,
> her honor to contempt.
> The shame of her fall matched the greatness of her
>   renown,
> and her pride was bowed low in grief.

King Antiochus then issued a decree throughout his empire that all his subjects were to become one people and abandon their own laws and religion. The nations everywhere complied with the royal command, and many in Yisrael accepted Greek idolatry, sacrificing to idols and profaning the *Shabbos*. Moreover, the king sent agents with written orders to Yerushalayim and the towns of Judea, decreeing the introduction of Greek practices and customs foreign to the Jews. Burnt-offerings, sacrifices, and libations in the Temple were forbidden; *Shabbos* and *Yamim Tovim* were to be profaned; the Temple and its *Cohanim* and *Leviim* were to be rendered unclean. Altars, idols, and "sacred" precincts were to be established; swine and other unclean animals were to be offered in sacrifice. The Jews were forbidden to circumcise their sons; they were ordered to make themselves abominable, unclean, and profane in every way, and to abandon the Torah and change all their laws. The penalty for disobedience was death.

Such was the decree which the king issued to all his subjects. He appointed superintendents over all the people, and instructed each town of Judea to offer a sacrifice, town by town. People joined them in large numbers, every one of them a traitor to the Torah. Their wicked conduct throughout the land drove the observant Jews to hide in every possible place of refuge.

On the fifteenth day of the month Kislev in the year 145, 'the abomination of desolation' was set up on the altar. Pagan altars were built throughout the towns of Judea; incense was offered at the doors of houses and in the streets. All Torah scrolls that were found were torn apart and burned. Anyone discovered in possession of a Torah scroll, or conforming to the Torah, was put to death by the king's sentence. Thus month after month these wicked men exercised their power against the Jews of their towns.

On the twenty-fifth day of the month of Kislev the overseers offered sacrifices on the pagan altar, which was placed on top of the Temple altar. In accordance with the royal decree, they executed women who had had their children circumcised. Their babies, their families, and those who had circumcised them were hanged. However, many in Yisrael found strength to resist, taking a determined stand against eating any unkosher food. They welcomed death rather than defile themselves and profane the holy Torah's covenant, and so they died. The anger of God was raging against Yisrael.

---

the year 145: 167 BCE

Chapter 2:
The Revolt Begins

At this time Mattisyahu, son of Yochanan, son of Shimon, achieved prominence. He was a priest of the family of Yehoyariv, from Yerushalayim, who had settled in Modi'in. Mattisyahu had five sons: Yochanan, called Gaddi; Shimon, called Tarsi; Yehudah, called Maccabee; Eleazar, called Avaran; and Yonasan, called Chapush.

When Mattisyahu witnessed the sacrilegious acts committed in Judea and Yerushalayim, he cried:

'Oh! Why was I born to see
my people crushed, the ruin of our holy city?
We sat idly by when it was surrendered,
when our holy place was given up to the aliens.
Her Temple is like a man robbed of honor;
its glorious vessels are carried off as spoil.
Her infants are slain in the street,
her young men by the sword of the foe.
Is there a nation that has not usurped her sovereignty,
a people that has not plundered her?
She has been stripped of all her adornment,
no longer free, but a slave.

Now that we have seen our Temple, with all its beauty and splendor, ruined and profaned by the Greeks, why should we continue to live?'

So Mattisyahu and his sons tore their garments, put on sackcloth, and mourned bitterly.

---

usurped her sovereignty: or, "occupied her palaces."

The king's officers in charge of enforcing apostasy came to the town of Modi'in to see that the pig sacrifice was offered. Many Jews allied themselves with them, but Mattisyahu and his sons stood separately in a group. The king's officers spoke to Mattisyahu: 'You are a leader here,' they said, 'a man of honor and influence in this town, with your sons and brothers behind you. Therefore you should be the first to come forward and carry out the king's order. All the nations have done so, as well as the leading men in Judea and the people left in Yerushalayim. You and your sons will be counted among the king's friends; you will all receive high honors, rich rewards of silver and gold, and many benefits.'

Mattisyahu replied to this offer in a resolute voice: 'Though all the nations of the king's dominions obey him and forsake their ancestral worship—though they have chosen to submit to his commands—yet I and my sons and brothers will follow the covenant of our fathers. Heaven forbid that we ever abandon the Torah and its statutes! We will not obey the king's command, nor will we deviate one step from the way of worship our tradition teaches.'

As soon as he had finished, a Jew stepped forward in full view of all to offer sacrifice on the pagan altar at Modi'in, in obedience to the royal command. The sight stirred Mattisyahu to indignation: he shook with passion, and in a fury of righteous anger rushed forward and slaughtered the traitor at the altar. At the same time he killed the Greek officer sent by the king to enforce the sacrifice, and pulled the pagan altar down. Thus Mattisyahu showed his fervent zeal for the Torah, just as Pinchas had done by killing Zimri ben Salu. 'Follow me!' he shouted through the town, 'every one of you who is dedicated to the Torah and strives to maintain the covenant.' He and his sons took to the hills, leaving all their belongings behind in the town.

At that time many who were dedicated to their religion and to Torah observance went down to the desert to live there. They took their children, their wives, and their cattle with them, for their miseries [at home] were unbearable. Word soon reached the king's officers and the forces in Yerushalayim, the city of David, that men who defied the king's order had fled into hiding-places in the desert. A large contingent of soldiers pursued them, and upon approaching them occupied positions opposite. They prepared to attack them on the *Shabbos*. 'There is still time,' the soldiers shouted. 'Come out, obey the king's command, and your lives will be spared.' 'We will not come out,' the Jews replied. 'We will not obey the king's command, nor will we profane the *Shabbos*.' Immediately the attack was launched, but the Jews did not retaliate; they neither hurled stones nor barricaded their caves. 'Let us all face death with a clear conscience,' they said. 'We call heaven and earth to testify that there is no justice in this slaughter.' So they were attacked and massacred on the *Shabbos*—men, women, and children, up to a thousand in all, and their cattle with them.

Mattisyahu and his friends were overwhelmed with grief when they heard the news. They said to one another, 'If we all do as our brothers have done, refusing to fight the Greeks for our lives as well as for our Torah's laws and customs, then they will soon wipe us off the face of the earth.' That day they decided that if anyone came to fight against them on the *Shabbos*, they would fight back, rather than all die as their brothers in the caves had done.

It was then that they were joined by a company of *Hassidim*—stalwarts of Yisrael, every one of them closely bound to the Torah. All who fled the atrocities came to swell

---

They took... making this a permanent move

their numbers, and thus increased their strength. Now that they had an organized force, they turned their wrath on the guilty men and Jewish renegades. Those who escaped their fierce attacks took refuge with the Greeks.

Mattisyahu and his friends then swept through the country, pulling down the pagan altars and forcibly circumcising all the uncircumcised babies found within the frontiers of [Eretz] Yisrael. They hunted down their arrogant enemies, and they prevailed. Thus they saved the Torah from the Greeks and their king, and broke the power of the tyrant Antiochus.

As Mattisyahu approached death he spoke to his sons: 'Arrogance still stands secure and renders judgment against us; it is a time of calamity and raging fury. But now, my sons, be zealous for the Torah, and give your lives for your fathers' covenant with it. Remember the deeds they did in their generations; great glory and eternal fame shall be yours. Did not Avraham prove steadfast under trial, and so gain credit as a righteous man? Yosef kept the commandments, hard-pressed though he was, and became lord of Egypt. Pinchas, our father, never flagged in his zeal, and he received the covenant of an everlasting priesthood. Yehoshua kept the Torah and became a judge in Yisrael. Calev bore witness before the congregation of Yisrael, and a share in the land was his reward. David was a man of loyalty, and he was granted the throne of an everlasting kingdom. Eliyahu never flagged in his zeal for the Torah, and he was taken up to Heaven alive. Chananiah, Azariah, and Mishael had faith, and they were saved from the blazing furnace. Daniel was a man of integrity; he was rescued from

---

As Mattisyahu... this happened before the war was over, as is clear from the following speech

the lions' jaws. As generation succeeds generation, follow their example; for no one who trusts in Heaven will ever lack strength. Do not fear a wicked man's talk; all his success will end in filth and worms. Today he may be high in honor, but tomorrow there will be no trace of him, because he will have returned to the dust, and all his schemes will have come to nothing. But you, my sons, draw your courage and strength from the Torah, for by it you will win great glory.

'Here is Shimon, your brother. I know him to be wise in counsel: always listen to him, for he will be a father to you. Yehudah Maccabee has been strong and brave from boyhood; he will be your commander in the field, and fight his people's battles. Gather to your side all who observe the Torah, and avenge your people's wrongs. Repay the Greeks in their own coin, and always heed the Torah's commands.'

Then Mattisyahu blessed them, and died, and was gathered to his fathers. He died in the year 146, and was buried by his sons in the family tomb at Modi'in while all Yisrael mourned.

Chapter 3

Yehudah and Yonasan Take Command

Then Yehudah Maccabee became the leader in his father's place. He had the support of all his brothers and his father's followers, and they fought vigorously for Yisrael.

---

the year 146: 166 BCE

He enhanced his people's glory.
He wore his breastplate like a giant
and bound himself with weapons of war.
He fought battle after battle;
he guarded his army with his sword.
He was like a lion in his exploits,
like a lion's whelp roaring for prey.
He hunted and tracked down the lawless Hellenizers;
he attacked the enemies of his people.
The lawless cowered in fear of him;
all evil-doers were confounded.
He elevated the cause of freedom;
he angered many kings,
but Yaakov rejoiced in his deeds.
He passed through the towns of Judea;
he destroyed the godless there.
He turned God's wrath away from Yisrael;
his fame spread far and wide,
and he rallied a people close to destruction.
He is remembered forever in blessing.

Apollonius now collected a Greek force and a large contingent from Shomron to fight against Yisrael. When Yehudah heard of it, he marched out to meet him and defeated and killed him. Many of the Greeks fell, and the rest took flight. Among the arms they captured, Yehudah seized the sword of Apollonius, and used it in his battles for the rest of his life.

When Seron, who commanded the Greek army in Syria, heard that Yehudah had mustered a large force, consisting of all his loyal followers of military age, he said to himself, 'I will win a glorious reputation in the empire by making war on Yehudah and his followers, who defy the royal edict.' Seron was reinforced by a strong contingent of renegade Jews, who marched up to help him take vengeance on Yisrael. When he reached the narrow pass of Beth-Horon,

Yehudah advanced to meet him with a handful of men. When Yehudah's followers saw the host coming against them, they said to him, 'How can so few of us fight against so many? Besides, we have had nothing to eat all day, and we are exhausted.'

Yehudah replied: 'Many can easily be overpowered by a few—it makes no difference to Heaven; victory can be achieved by a few as easily as by many. Victory does not depend on numbers; strength comes from Heaven alone. Our enemies come filled with insolence and lawlessness to plunder and to kill us, our wives and children. But we are fighting for our lives and our Torah. Heaven will crush them before our eyes. You need not be afraid of them.'

When he had finished speaking, he launched a sudden attack, and Seron and his army broke before him. They pursued them down the pass of Beth-Horon as far as the plain. Some eight hundred of the enemy fell, and the rest fled to Philistia.

Following this startling victory, Yehudah and his brothers inspired fear in the Greeks, and alarm spread to all the Greeks surrounding them. His fame reached the ears of King Antiochus, for the story of his battles was told in every nation. When King Antiochus heard this news, he flew into a rage and assembled an immensely powerful army, representing all the forces of his empire. He opened his treasury and paid a year's wages to his troops, commanding them to be prepared for any duty. But he found that his resources were running low; his tribute, too, had dwindled as a result of the disaffection and violence he had brought upon the world by abolishing the Torah's traditions, laws, and customs. Alarmed, he realized he might be short of money (as had happened once or twice before) both for his normal expenses and for the gifts he had been accustomed to distribute more lavishly than any of his predecessors on the throne.

As a result of his financial difficulties, he decided to go to Persia, collect the tribute due from the provinces, and so raise a large sum of money. He left Lysias, a distinguished member of the royal family, as viceroy of the territories between the Euphrates and the Egyptian frontier. He also appointed him guardian of his son Antiochus until his return. He transferred half the armed forces to Lysias, including the war elephants, and told him all that he wanted done, especially to the population of Judea and Yerushalayim. He instructed Lysias to send a force to break and destroy the strength of Yisrael and those who were left in Yerushalayim, in order to blot out all memory of them from Yerushalayim and Judea. Antiochus commanded Lysias to settle foreigners in all the territory and allot Eretz Yisrael to these settlers. Then the king took the other half of his forces with him and set out from Antioch, his capital, in the year 147. He crossed the Euphrates and marched through the upper provinces.

Lysias chose Ptolemaeus, son of Dorymenes, with Nicanor and Gorgias—all three powerful members of the order of the King's Friends—and sent forty thousand infantry, with seven thousand cavalry, to invade Judea and devastate the country as the king had commanded. They set out with all their forces and encamped near Emmaus in the lowlands. The Syrian Greek merchants of the region, impressed by what they heard of the army, took a large quantity of silver and gold, with a supply of chains, and came into the camp to buy Israelites for slaves. The army was also reinforced by troops from Syria and Philistia.

---

the year 147: 165 BCE

With the enemy encamped within their frontiers, Yehudah and his brothers saw that their situation was perilous. They learned, too, of the commands which the king had given for the complete destruction of the Jewish nation. So they said to one another, 'Let us restore the shattered fortunes of our nation; let us fight for our nation and for the *Beis HaMikdash*.' They gathered in full assembly to prepare for battle, and to pray and seek Divine mercy and compassion.

> Yerushalayim lay deserted like a wilderness;
> none of her children came or went.
> Her holy place was trampled down;
> aliens and heathen lodged in her citadel.
> Joy had been banished from Jacob,
> and flute and harp were silent.

They assembled at Mitzpah, opposite Yerushalayim, which had been a former place of worship for Yisrael. That day they fasted, put on sackcloth, sprinkled ashes on their heads, and tore their garments. They unrolled the Torah scroll, seeking the guidance which Greeks seek from the images of their gods. They brought the priestly vestments and offered the first-fruits, and the tithes; they presented *Nezirim* who had completed their vows, and they cried to Heaven: 'What shall we do with these *Nezirim*, and where shall we take them? Your holy *Mikdash* is trampled and defiled, and sorrow and humiliation have come upon Your priests. And see, the Greeks have gathered against us to destroy us. You know the fate they plan for us; how can we withstand them unless You help us?' Then the trumpets sounded, and a great shout went up.

Nezirim: men under a special vow of abstinence; see. *Bemidbar* ch. 6.

Yehudah then appointed leaders of the people: officers over thousands, hundreds, fifties, and tens. As the Torah commands, he ordered back to their homes those who were building their houses or planting new vineyards, the newly-wed, and those who were faint-hearted. Thereupon, the army moved and took up positions to the south of Emmaus, where Yehudah addressed them: 'Prepare for action and show yourselves men. Be ready at dawn to fight these Greeks, who are massed against us to destroy us and our holy *Mikdash*. Better die fighting than look on while calamity overwhelms our people and the holy *Mikdash*. But it will be as Heaven wills.'

Chapter 4
The First Battle

Gorgias, taking a detachment of five thousand men and a thousand picked cavalry, set out by night, with guides who were men from the citadel, to attack the Jewish army and surprise them. But Yehudah had word of this plan, and he and his soldiers moved out to attack the king's army in Emmaus while its forces were still divided. Gorgias reached Yehudah's camp during the night, but found no one there. So he set out to search for them in the hills, assuming that 'these Jews are running away from us.'

At daybreak Yehudah was in the plain with only three thousand men, who were not even fully equipped with swords and armor. They saw the Greeks' camp strongly fortified with breastworks, while mounted guards, seasoned troops, patrolled around it.

Yehudah said to his men: 'Do not be afraid of their great numbers, nor panic when they charge. Remember how our fathers were saved at the Red Sea, when Paroh and his army were pursuing them. Let us cry now to Heaven to favor our cause, to remember the covenant of Torah that *God* made with our fathers, and to crush this army before us today. Then all the Greeks will know that *God* saves and liberates Yisrael.'

When the Greeks looked up and saw the Jews advancing to the attack, they marched out of their camp to give battle. Yehudah and his men sounded their trumpets and closed in on them. The Greeks broke and fled to the plain—all their troops towards the rear fell by the sword. The Jews pursued the enemy as far as Gezer and the lowlands of Ekron, Ashdod, and Yavneh, inflicting about three thousand casualties.

Yehudah and his force then ceased the pursuit and returned to the battlefield. He said to the people: 'Curb your greed for spoil; there is more fighting before us. Gorgias and his force are in the hills nearby. Stand firm now against our enemies and fight; after that, plunder as you please.'

Before Yehudah had finished speaking, an enemy patrol appeared, reconnoitering from the hills. The Greeks saw that their army was in flight and that their camp was being set on fire; they were panic-stricken when they saw the smoke, and when they saw the army of Yehudah in the plain, ready for battle, they all fled to Philistia.

Then Yehudah turned back to plunder the Greek camp, where they found much gold and silver, violet- and purple-dyed goods, and great riches. On their return they sang

---

Ekron: a best guess; the text reads "Edom," which makes no sense.

violet- and purple-dyed goods: which were very precious—"Tyrian purple" was the most expensive dye in the world.

songs of thanksgiving and praised Heaven, 'for it is good, because His mercy endures for ever'. That day represented a great deliverance for Yisrael.

Those Greeks who managed to escape reported to Lysias all that had happened. He was overwhelmed with disappointment, because Israel had not suffered the disaster he had hoped for, nor had he fulfilled the orders of King Antiochus.

During the following year Lysias gathered sixty thousand picked infantry and five thousand cavalry to make war on the Jews. They marched into Edom and encamped at Beit Tzur, where Yehudah met them with ten thousand men. When he saw the strength of the enemy's army, he prayed: 'All praise to You, Savior of Yisrael, who broke the attack of the giant Goliath through Your servant David. You delivered the army of the Philistines into the power of Saul's son Yonasan and his armor-bearer. Just so, put the Greek army into the power of Your people Yisrael. Humble their pride in their forces and their mounted men. Strike them with panic, turn their insolent strength to water, make them reel under a crushing defeat. Overthrow them by the sword of those who love you, and let all who know Your name praise You with songs of thanksgiving.'

So the battle began, and Lysias lost about five thousand men in the close fighting. When he saw his own army routed and Yehudah's army full of daring, ready to live or die nobly, he departed for Antioch and there collected a force of mercenaries, in order to return to Judea with a much larger army even than before.

But Yehudah and his brothers, eager to give thanks to God for their deliverance, said: 'Now that our enemies have been crushed, let us go up to Yerushalayim to cleanse the

Beis HaMikdash and rededicate it.' So the whole army was assembled and went up to Mount Zion. There they found the *Beis HaMikdash* destroyed, the altar profaned, the gates burned down, the courts overgrown and thick with vegetation, and the priests' rooms in ruin. They tore their garments, wailed loudly, put ashes on their heads, and fell on their faces to the ground. They sounded the ceremonial trumpets, and cried aloud to Heaven.

Then Yehudah detailed troops to engage the garrison of the citadel while he cleansed the *Beis HaMikdash*. He selected priests who were without blemish, devoted to the Torah, and they purified the *Beis HaMikdash*, removing the stones of the altar which defiled it and discarding them in an unclean place. They discussed what to do with the altar of burnt-offering, which was profaned, and rightly decided to demolish it, for fear it might become a standing reproach to them because it had been defiled by the Greeks. They therefore dismantled the altar and stored away the stones in a fitting place on *Har HaBayis*, until a prophet should arise who could be consulted about them. They took unhewn stones, as the Torah commands, and built a new altar on the model of the previous one. They rebuilt the *Beis HaMikdash* and restored its interior, and consecrated the Temple courts. They renewed the sacred vessels and the *Menorah*, and brought the altar of incense and the table into the *Beis HaMikdash*. They burned incense on the altar and lit the lamps of the *Menorah* to shine within the *Beis HaMikdash*. When they had put the Bread of the Presence on the table and hung the *Paroches*, all their work was completed.

Then, early on the twenty-fifth day of the ninth month,

Har HaBayis: the Temple Mount

the month of Kislev, in the year 148, sacrifice was offered as the Torah commands on the newly-made altar of burnt-offering. On the anniversary of the day when the Greeks had profaned it, on that very day it was rededicated, with hymns of thanksgiving, to the music of harps and lutes and cymbals. All the people prostrated themselves, worshipping and praising Heaven that their cause had prospered.

They celebrated the rededication of the altar for eight days; there was great rejoicing as they brought burnt-offerings and sacrificed peace-offerings and thank-offerings. They decorated the front of the *Beis HaMikdash* with golden wreaths and ornamental shields. They renewed the gates and the priests' rooms, and fitted them with doors. With great merry-making the people rejoiced that they were cleansed of the disgrace inflicted upon them by the Greeks.

Then Yehudah, his brothers, and the whole congregation of Yisrael decreed that the rededication of the altar should be observed with joy and gladness at the same season each year, for eight days, beginning on the twenty-fifth of Kislev.

At that time they encircled Mount Zion with high walls and strong towers to prevent the Greeks from coming and trampling it down as they had done before. Yehudah set a garrison there; he also fortified Beit Tzur, so that the people should have a fortress facing Edom.

---

the year 148: 164 BCE

Chapter 5
Retaliation

When the Greeks heard that the altar had been rebuilt and the *Beis HaMikdash* rededicated, they were furious and determined to wipe out all those of the race of Yaakov who lived among them. Thus began the work of massacre and extermination among the people.

Yehudah then made war on the descendants of Eisav in Edom and attacked Acrabattene, because they had constricted Yisrael's borders. The Edomites suffered a severe and humiliating defeat, and Yehudah took spoils from them. He also remembered the wrong done by the Baeanites, who with their traps and road-blocks were continually ambushing the Israelites. He first confined them to their forts and took up positions against them; then he swore to destroy them and set the forts ablaze with all their occupants. He crossed over to the Ammonites and came upon a strong and numerous force under the command of a certain Timotheus. He fought many battles with them, and they broke before him and were crushed. After capturing Jazer and its dependent villages, he returned to Judea.

Then the Greeks in Gilead gathered against the Israelites within their territory, intending to destroy them; but they took refuge in the fortress of Dathema, and sent this letter to Yehudah and his brothers:

> The Greeks around us have gathered to wipe us out. They are preparing to come and seize the fortress where we have taken refuge; Timotheus is in command of their army. So come at once and rescue us from their clutches, for many of our number have al-

ready fallen. All our fellow-Jews in the region of Tubias have been massacred, their wives and their children taken captive, and their property carried off. About a thousand men there have lost their lives.

While the letter was being read, other messengers, with their garments torn from mourning, arrived from the Galil. 'Ptolemais, Tyre and Sidon,' they said, 'and all the gentiles in the Galil, have mustered their forces to make an end of us.'

When Yehudah and the people heard this, a full assembly was called to decide what they should do for their fellow-countrymen in distress under enemy attack. Yehudah said to Shimon his brother, 'Choose your men, and go and rescue your countrymen in Galil, while I and my brother Yonasan will march into Gilead.' The rest of his forces he left for the defences of Judea, with Yosef ben Zechariah and Azariah, leading citizens, and he gave them this order: 'Take charge of the people of Yerushalayim, but on no account join battle with the Greeks until we return.' Shimon was allotted three thousand men for the march on the Galil, and Yehudah eight thousand for the march on Gilead.

Shimon invaded the Galil and, after many battles, broke the resistance of the Greeks. He pursued them as far as the gate of Ptolemais, killing nearly three thousand of them, and stripped their corpses. He returned with the Jews from Galil and Arbatta, their wives and children, and all their property, and brought them to Judea with great jubilation.

Meanwhile Yehudah Maccabee and his brother Yonasan crossed the Jordan and marched for three days through the desert. They came upon some Nabataeans, who met them peacefully. Yehudah gave them an account of all that had happened to their fellow-Jews in Gilead, many of whom were being held prisoner in Batzrah and Betzer, in Alemah,

Casphor, Maked, and Karnaim, all large fortified towns, and some in the other towns of Gilead. 'Your enemies', the Nabateans told the brothers, 'are marshalling their forces to storm your fortresses tomorrow so as to capture them and destroy all the Jews in them in a single day.'

So Yehudah and his army suddenly turned aside to Batzrah by way of the desert, captured the town, and put all the males to the sword. He plundered all their property and set fire to the town. From there he made a night-march and came within reach of the fortress of Dathema. When dawn broke they saw before them an innumerable host, bringing up scaling-ladders and siege-engines to capture the fortress from the Jewish defenders. Yehudah saw that the battle had already started, and a cry went up to Heaven from the town, with trumpeting and loud shouting. Yehudah said to his men: 'Now is the time to fight for our brothers.'

They marched out in three columns to take the enemy in the rear, then sounded the trumpets and cried aloud in prayer. When the army of Timotheus recognized that it was Yehudah Maccabee, they fled before him. Yehudah totally defeated them, and nearly eight thousand of the enemy fell on that single day.

Yehudah then turned aside to Alema, attacked and captured it, and killed all the males. He plundered the town and set it on fire. From there he moved on and occupied Casphor, Maked, Betzer, and the other towns of Gilead.

After these events Timotheus gathered another army, taking up positions opposite Raphon on the other side of the ravine. Yehudah sent spies to their camp who reported that all the Greeks in the neighborhood, in addition to hired Arab mercenaries, had rallied in great numbers to Timotheus. They were encamped on the far side of the ravine, ready to engage Yehudah in battle. In response, Yehudah marched out to meet them.

As Yehudah and his army were approaching the flooded ravine, Timotheus said to his officers: 'If Yehudah crosses over to our side first, we will not be able to stand up to him; he will certainly get the better of us. If, however, his courage fails him and he takes up a position on the other side of the river, then we will cross over and get the better of him.' When Yehudah reached the ravine, he stationed his trained officers on its bank, with instructions that no one should be allowed to take up a fixed position, but all should advance to battle. Thus Yehudah forestalled the enemy by crossing to attack them, with all his people following. The Greeks broke before him, discarding their arms and taking refuge in the temple at Karnaim. But Yehudah captured the town and burned the temple together with all its occupants. Karnaim was completely subdued and could no longer withstand him.

Then Yehudah gathered together all the Israelites in Gilead and escorted them to Judea—an immense host of young and old, men, women, and children, and all their property. On the road they came as far as Ephron, a large and strongly fortified town which was impossible to circumvent. The only route was through the town, but the townsmen kept them out, barricading their gates with boulders. Yehudah sent them a conciliatory message: 'We have to pass through your territory to reach our own. We shall only march through, and no one will harm you.' But they refused to open their gates.

Yehudah issued orders to the whole host for everyone to halt where he was. Then the fighting men took up battle positions and attacked the town all that day and all the night, until it was theirs. They killed every male, razed the town to the ground, plundered it, and then marched through it over the bodies of the dead. They crossed the Jordan to the great plain opposite Beit Shean, while Yehudah brought up the stragglers and encouraged the people all along the road, till he arrived in Judea. They went up to Mount Zion, the *Beis HaMikdash,* with gladness and jubilation, and offered burnt-offerings for having returned in safety without the loss of a single life.

While Yehudah and Yonasan were in Gilead, and Shimon their brother in Galil was besieging Ptolemais, the two commanders, Yosef ben Zechariah and Azariah, heard of their exploits in battle. 'We too', they said, 'must make a name for ourselves: let us go and fight the Greeks in our neighborhood.' So they gave orders to their forces and marched against Yavneh. Gorgias came out of the town with his men to engage them in battle—and Yosef and Azariah were routed, pursued to the frontier of Judea with the subsequent loss that day of about two thousand lives. The Israelites thus suffered a heavy defeat because their commanders, eager for glory, had not obeyed Yehudah and his brothers, whose family had been chosen to bring deliverance to Yisrael.

Yehudah and his brothers were renowned both in all Yisrael and among the Greeks; wherever their fame was known, crowds flocked to acclaim them.

After this Yehudah marched with his brothers and made war on the descendants of Esau to the south. He smote Chevron and its villages, demolished its fortifications, and burned down all its forts. He then set out to invade Philistine territory, marching through Marisa. On that day several priests, who had ill-advisedly gone into action wishing to distinguish themselves, fell in battle. The Jews turned aside to Ashdod in Philistia. Yehudah pulled down their altars, burned the images of their gods, plundered their towns, and returned to Judea.

Chapter 6
The Death of Antiochus

As King Antiochus marched through the upper provinces he heard that there was a city in Persia called Elymais, famous for its wealth in silver and gold. Its temple was very rich, full of gold shields, coats of mail, and arms, left there by Alexander son of Philip, king of Macedon and the first to be king over the Greeks. Antiochus tried to capture and plunder the city but failed because his plan had become known to the citizens. They resisted successfully, and he withdrew to Babylon in bitter disappointment.

A messenger met Antiochus in Persia with the news that the armies which had invaded Judea were in full retreat. He was informed that Lysias had advanced with an exceptionally strong force, only to be flung back before the enemy. The Jews had increased their strength by capturing arms, equipment, and spoils from the Greek armies they had defeated. They had pulled down the abomination Antiochus had built on the altar in Yerushalayim, and surrounded the *Beis HaMikdash* with high walls, the way it had been before he had fortified Beit Tzur.

When the king heard this news he was so furious that he took to his bed, ill with grief at the defeat of his plans. There he lay for many days, his bitter grief repeatedly overwhelming him until he realized that he was dying. He summoned all his friends and said to them: 'I am unable to sleep; the weight of my burden has broken my heart. At first I said to myself, "Why am I overwhelmed by this flood of trouble, I who was kind and well-loved at the height of my power?"

But now I remember the wrong I did in Jerusalem, when I took all her vessels of silver and gold, and when I made an unjust attempt to wipe out the inhabitants of Judea. It is for this, I know, that these misfortunes have come upon me; and here I am, dying of grief in a foreign land.'

He summoned Philip, one of the King's Friends, and appointed him regent over his whole empire, giving him the crown and the royal robe and signet-ring, with authority to take his son Antiochus and raise him to be king. King Antiochus died in Persia in the year 149.

When Lysias learned that the king was dead, he placed the young Antiochus (whom he had reared from boyhood) on the throne to succeed his father, and gave him the name of Eupator.

Meanwhile the garrison of the citadel were confining the Israelites to the neighborhood of the *Beis HaMikdash*, and giving continual support to the Greeks by their harassing tactics. Yehudah therefore determined to deal with them accordingly. He gathered all the people together to lay siege to the citadel in the year 150, erecting emplacements and siege-engines against the enemy.

Some of the besieged garrison managed to escape and were joined by a number of renegade Israelites. They went to the king and said: 'How long must we wait for you to do justice and avenge our comrades? We were willing to serve your father, to follow his instructions and to obey his decrees, and what was the result? Our own countrymen became our enemies. They actually killed as many of us as

---

the year 149: 163 BCE
the year 150: 162 BCE

they could find, and robbed us of our property. Nor are we the only ones to suffer at their hands. They have attacked all their neighbors as well. At this very moment they are besieging the citadel in Jerusalem and expect to capture it; they have also fortified both the Temple and Beit Tzur. Unless Your Majesty quickly overpowers them, they will achieve even further objectives, and you will not be able to keep them in check.'

When the king heard this he was furious. He assembled all his Friends, the commanders of his army, and his cavalry officers. He was joined by mercenary troops from other kingdoms and from the islands. His forces numbered one hundred thousand infantry, twenty thousand cavalry, and thirty-two war elephants. They passed through Edom and laid siege to Beit Tzur. They kept up the attack for a long time and erected siege-engines, but the Jewish defenders made a sortie, setting fire to them and fighting back vigorously.

Yehudah now withdrew from the citadel and encamped at Beit Zechariah, opposite the camp of the king. Early next morning the king broke camp and rushed his army along the road to Beit Zechariah, where his forces were drawn up for battle. The trumpets were sounded, the elephants were prepared for battle by feeding with the juice of grapes and of mulberries. The great beasts were distributed among the phalanxes, each consisting of a thousand men equipped with mail coats and bronze helmets. Five hundred picked horsemen were also assigned to each animal, and wherever it went they went with it. Each animal had a strong wooden turret fastened on its back with a harness for protection, and carried four fighting men as well as an Indian driver. The

---

the juice of grapes... as a stimulant, to drive the beasts into a frenzy

rest of the cavalry Lysias stationed on either flank of the army, to harass the enemy while they themselves were protected by the phalanxes. When the sun shone on the gold and bronze shields, they flashed like torches and lit up the hills.

Part of the king's army was deployed over the heights and part over the low ground, advancing with precision and confidence. All who heard the din of this marching multitude and its clashing arms shook with fear at the sound of the great and powerful army.

Yehudah advanced with his army and attacked, killing six hundred of the king's men. Eleazar Avaran, seeing that one of the elephants wore royal armor and stood out above all the rest, thought that the king was riding on it. So he gave his life to save his people and win everlasting renown for himself. He ran boldly towards it, into the middle of the phalanx, dealing death right and left, while the soldiers fell back on either side before him. He ran underneath the elephant, thrusting his sword at it from below and killing it. It collapsed on top of him, and there he died.

When the Jews saw the strength and confidence of the imperial forces in full equipage, they retreated before them. Part of the king's army marched up to Yerushalayim to renew the battle, and the king brought Judea and Mount Zion under siege. He made peace with the inhabitants of Beit Tzur, who abandoned the town, having no more food there to withstand a siege, since it was *shemittah* year and the land lay fallow. So the king occupied Beit Tzur and detailed a garrison to hold it.

He then attacked the *Beis HaMikdash* and subjected it to a long siege, setting up emplacements, siege engines with flamethrowers, and catapults for discharging stones, barbed missiles, and slings. But the defenders, too, constructed engines to counter his engines, and put up a prolonged resistance. There was no food, however, in the Temple because of the *shemittah* year, and because those who from time to time had arrived in Judea as refugees from the Greeks had eaten up all that remained of the provisions. The famine had been so severe that only a few men were left in the Temple, the rest having scattered to their own homes.

Lysias heard that Philip, whom King Antiochus had appointed before he died to educate his son Antiochus for the kingship, had returned from Persia and Media with the late king's expeditionary force, and that he was seeking to take over the government. He quickly issued orders to depart, telling the king, his commanders, and his troops: 'Every day we are growing weaker, provisions are low, the place we are besieging is strong, and the affairs of the empire are pressing. So let us offer these men terms and make peace with them and their whole nation. Let us guarantee their right to follow their laws and customs as they used to do, for it was our abolition of these very customs and laws that fueled their resentment, and produced all these consequences.'

The proposal met with the approval of the king and the commanders, and an offer of peace was sent and accepted. The king and his commanders bound themselves by oath, and on the agreed terms the besieged emerged from their stronghold. But when the king entered Mount Zion and saw how strongly the place was fortified, he went back on the oath he had sworn, and gave orders for the surrounding wall to be demolished. He then set off at top speed for Antioch, where he found Philip in possession; a battle ensued, and the city was taken by storm.

Chapter 7
The Renegades

Meanwhile—in the year 151—Demetrius son of Seleucus left Rome, landed with a handful of men at a town on the coast, and there made himself king. While he was traveling to the royal seat of his ancestors, the Syrian army seized Antiochus and Lysias, intending to hand them over to Demetrius. When this was reported to him he said, 'Do not let me set eyes on them.' The soldiers accordingly put them to death, and Demetrius ascended the throne in Damascus.

All the godless renegades of Yisrael, led by Alcimus, who aspired to be High Priest, came to King Demetrius and brought charges against their people. They told him: 'Yehudah and his brothers have killed all your supporters, and have driven us from our country. Please send a man whom you trust to observe the devastation they have inflicted upon us and upon the king's territory, and punish them and all their supporters.' The king chose Bacchides, one of the King's Friends, who was governor beyond the Euphrates, a man of high standing in the empire and loyal to the king. He sent him and the godless Alcimus, on whom he had conferred the high-priesthood, with orders to take vengeance on Israel.

They set out with a large army and entered Judea. Bacchides sent envoys to Yehudah and his brothers to make false offers of friendship; but when they saw what a large force Bacchides had brought with him, they disregarded these offers.

---

the year 151: 161 BCE

A delegation of *talmidei chachamim* met with Alcimus and Bacchides asking for fair treatment. These *Hassidim* were in fact the first group in Yisrael to make overtures to the two, assuming, as they said to themselves, 'A priest of the family of Aharon has come with their forces, and he will do us no harm.' The language of Alcimus was conciliatory, assuring them on oath that no harm was intended to them or their friends. But once he had gained their confidence, he arrested sixty of them and put them to death in a single day; as Scripture says:

> 'The bodies of Your *tzaddikim* were scattered about;
> their blood was shed around Yerushalayim,
> and there was none to bury them.'

This act terrified the people, who agreed, 'There is neither truth nor justice among the Greeks; they have broken their pledge and the oath they swore.' Then Bacchides left Yerushalayim and camped in Beit Zayit, where he ordered the arrest of many of those who had deserted to him. He had them slaughtered and thrown into a great pit together with some of the local people. Bacchides assigned the whole district to Alcimus, detailed some troops to assist him, and returned to King Demetrius.

Alcimus fought hard for his high-priesthood. All the trouble-making Hellenizers rallied to him. They gained control over Judea and did terrible damage in Yisrael. When Yehudah saw all the mischief that Alcimus and his followers had brought upon the Israelites, far worse than anything the Greeks had done, he marched through all the territory of Judea and its environs, punishing Jewish deserters and restricting their access to the country districts. When Alcimus saw that Yehudah and his band had grown powerful, and recognized that he was unable to withstand them, he returned to the king and accused them of atrocities.

Then the king sent Nicanor, one of his distinguished commanders and a bitter enemy of Yisrael, with orders to exterminate them. Nicanor arrived at Yerushalayim with a large force, and sent envoys to Yehudah and his brothers to make false offers of friendship: 'Let us not quarrel,' he said; 'I propose to come with a few men for a friendly personal meeting.'

He came to Yehudah, and although they greeted one another as friends, yet Nicanor was preparing to kidnap Yehudah. But Yehudah discovered that Nicanor's visit was a trick and refused to meet him again. Nicanor, realizing that his plan had been detected, marched out to battle Yehudah near Kefar Shalom. About five hundred of Nicanor's army were killed, and the rest escaped to the city of David.

After these events Nicanor went up to Mount Zion, where some of the priests and *dayanim* of the Sanhedrin came out from the *Mikdash* to give him a friendly welcome, and to show him the burnt-offering which was being sacrificed for the king. But Nicanor mocked them and spat on them, boasting and swearing angrily: 'Unless Yehudah and his army are surrendered to me at once, when I return victorious I will burn down this house.' And he went off in a rage. After his tirade the priests went in and stood facing the altar and the *Kodesh*. They wept and said: 'You chose this house to bear Your name, to be a house of prayer and supplication for Your people. Take vengeance on this man and his army, and make them fall by the sword. Remember all their blasphemy, and grant them no reprieve.'

---

spat on them: literally, "polluted them"

Kodesh: the inner chambers of the Temple, where the incense altar, Menorah, and Ark stood

Nicanor moved from Yerushalayim and encamped at Beth Horon, where he was joined by the Greek army from Syria. Yehudah encamped at Hadassah with three thousand men, and there he prayed in these words: 'There was a king whose followers blasphemed, and Your angel came forth and struck down one hundred and eighty-five thousand of them. So please crush this army before us today, and let all men know that Nicanor has reviled Your Holy place; judge him as his wickedness deserves.'

The armies joined battle on the thirteenth of the month of Adar, and the army of Nicanor suffered a crushing defeat, he himself being the first to fall in the battle. When his army saw that Nicanor had fallen, they threw away their arms and fled. The Jews, sounding the signal trumpets in the enemy's rear, pursued them as far as Gezer, a day's journey from Hadassah. From all the villages of Judea the inhabitants came out and attacked the enemy's flanks, forcing them back upon their pursuers. They all fell by the sword and there were no survivors. The Jews seized spoil and booty; they cut off Nicanor's head and that right hand which he had stretched out so arrogantly, and brought them to be displayed at Yerushalayim. There was great public rejoicing and that day was kept as a special day of jubilation. It was ordained that the day should be observed annually, on the thirteenth of Adar. Thus Judea enjoyed a short period of peace.

Chapter 8
Enter the Romans

Meanwhile Yehudah had heard about the Romans, who were renowned for their military power and for the welcome they gave those who became their allies; any who joined them could be sure of their firm friendship. He was told about the wars they had fought, and the valor they had shown in their conquest of the Gauls, who now paid them tribute. He heard of their successes in Spain, where they had seized silver and gold mines, establishing a hold on the entire country—distant as it was from their own land—with their patience and good judgment. There were kings from far and near who had marched against them; those who had not suffered crushing defeats paid them annual tribute.

They had crushed in battle and conquered Philip, Perseus king of Kittim, and all who had attacked them. Antiochus, the great king of Asia, had marched against them with one hundred and twenty elephants, with cavalry and chariots and an immense force, but they had totally defeated him. They had taken the king alive, and had required that he and his successors should pay them a large annual tribute, give hostages, and cede the territories of India, Media, and Lydia, together with some of their finest provinces. These they had taken from him and given to King Eumenes.

When the Greeks planned to attack and destroy them, they heard of it and sent a single general against them. During the battle many of the Greeks fell; the Romans took their women and children prisoner, plundered their territory and annexed it, razed their fortifications, and made them subjects, as they are to this day. They destroyed or made tributary the remaining kingdoms, the islands, and all who opposed them. With their friends, however, and all who put themselves under their protection, they maintained a firm friendship.

They thus conquered kings near and far, and all who heard their fame were in fear of them. Those whom they wished to help and to appoint as kings, became kings, and those they wished to depose, they deposed; and thus they rose to great heights of power. Despite all this power, not one of them made any personal claim to greatness by wearing a crown or donning the royal purple. They had established a senate where three hundred and twenty senators met daily to deliberate, giving careful and constant consideration to properly maintaining the affairs of the common people. They entrusted their government and the ruling of all their territory to a different one of their number every year, all obeying this one man without envy or jealousy.

Accordingly, Yehudah chose Eupolemus ben Yochanan ben Accos and Jason ben Eleazar, and sent them to Rome to conclude a treaty of friendship and alliance, so that the Romans might rid them of tyranny, for it was clear that the Greek empire was slowly reducing Yisrael to slavery. They made the long journey to Rome and entered the Senate, where they spoke as follows: 'Judas, known as Maccabaeus, his brothers, and the Jewish people have sent us to you to conclude a treaty of friendly alliance with you, so that we may be enrolled as your allies and friends.' The Romans found the proposal acceptable, and the following is a copy of the reply which they inscribed on tablets of bronze and sent to Yerushalayim, so that the Jews there might have a record of the treaty of alliance:

> 'Success to the Romans and the Jewish nation by sea and land for ever! May sword and foe be far from them! But if war breaks out first against Rome or any of her allies throughout her dominion, then the Jewish nation shall support them whole-heartedly as occasion may require. To the enemies of Rome or of her allies the Jews shall neither give nor supply provisions, arms, money, or ships; so Rome has decided; and they shall observe their commitments, without compensation.
>
> 'Similarly, if war breaks out first against the Jewish nation, then the Romans shall give them hearty support

as occasion may require. To their enemies shall be given neither provisions, arms, money, nor ships; so Rome has decided. These commitments shall be kept without breach of faith.'

These are the terms of the agreement which the Romans made with the Jewish people. But if, hereafter, both parties shall agree to add or to rescind anything, then they shall do as they decide; any such addition or rescindment shall be valid.

To this the Romans added: 'As for the misdeeds which King Demetrius is perpetrating against the Jews, we have written to him as follows: "Why have you oppressed our friends and allies the Jews so harshly? If they make any further complaint against you, then we will see that justice is done them, and will make war upon you by sea and by land."'

Chapter 9
The Death of Yehudah

When Demetrius heard that Nicanor and his forces had fallen in battle, he sent Bacchides and Alcimus a second time into Judea, with the right wing of his army. They marched along the Gilgal road, laid siege to Messaloth in Arbela, and captured it, inflicting heavy losses.

In the first month of the year 152, they moved their camp to Yerushalayim. From there they marched to Berea with twenty thousand infantry and two thousand cavalry. At the

---

the year 152: 160 BCE

time Yehudah was in camp at Alasa with three thousand picked men. But when they saw the size of the enemy forces their courage failed and many deserted, leaving a mere eight hundred men in the field.

When Yehudah saw that with the campaign going against him his army had deserted, his heart sank, for there was no time to rally them. Though much discouraged, he said to those who were left, 'Let us move to the attack and see if we can defeat them.' But his men tried to dissuade him: 'Impossible!' they said. 'No; let us save our lives now and come back later with our comrades to fight them. Now we are too few.' But Yehudah replied: 'Heaven forbid that I should do such a thing as run away! If our time is come, let us die bravely for our fellow-countrymen and leave no stain on our honor.'

The Syrian Greek army left its camp and assumed its position to meet the Jews. The Greek cavalry was divided into two detachments: the slingers and archers went ahead of the main force, and the veterans were in the front line. Bacchides was on the right. The phalanx came on in two divisions with trumpets sounding; Yehudah's men also sounded their trumpets. The earth shook with the roar of the armies as they engaged in battle, fighting from dawn until evening.

When Yehudah saw that Bacchides and the main strength of his army was on the right flank, all his stout-hearted men rallied to him, and they broke the Greek Syrian right; then he pursued them as far as Mount Ashdod. When the Syrians on the left wing saw that their right flank had been broken, they turned about and followed on the heels of Yehudah and his men, attacking them in the rear. The fighting became very heavy, and many fell on both sides.

Yehudah himself fell, and the rest of the Jews took flight.

Yonasan and Shimon carried off their brother Yehudah to bury him in the family tomb at Modi'in, and they wept over him. Great was the grief in Yisrael, who mourned him for many days, saying,

> 'How is our champion fallen,
> the savior of Yisrael!'

The rest of the history of Yehudah, his wars, exploits, and achievements—all these were so numerous that they have not been written down.

After the death of Yehudah the Hellenizing renegades surfaced in every part of Yisrael, and all the evil-doers reappeared. In those days a terrible famine broke out, causing the country to go over to their side. Bacchides chose apostates to be in control of the country. These men made inquiries and tracked down the friends of Yehudah and brought them before Bacchides, who took vengeance, heaping indignities on them and breaking their spirit. It was a time of great affliction for Yisrael, worse than any since the day when prophets ceased to appear among them. Then all the friends of Yehudah assembled and said to Yonasan: 'Since your brother Yehudah died, there has not been a man like him to take the lead against our enemies. Bacchides and those of our own nation are hostile to us. Today, therefore, we choose you to succeed him as our ruler and leader and to fight our battles.' So Yonasan took over the leadership at that time, in place of his brother Yehudah.

The news reached Bacchides, and he went out himself to kill Yonasan. When Yonasan and his brother Shimon and all their men learned of this, they took refuge in the desert of Tekoa, encamping by the pool of Asphar. Bacchides discovered this on Shabbos and crossed the Jordan with his whole army. So Yonasan sent his brother Yochanan to take the camp followers and appeal to his friends the Nabataeans to look after their baggage train, which was of some size. But the Jambrites appeared from the Medaba and kidnapped Yochanan, seized the baggage and made off with it.

Some time afterwards news was brought to Yonasan and his brother Shimon that the Jambrites were celebrating an important wedding, and bringing the bride, the daughter of one of the great nobles of Canaan, from Nadabath with a large retinue. Remembering how their brother Yochanan had been killed, Yonasan and his men set out and hid themselves under the cover of a hill. They looked out and saw the bridegroom, in the middle of a bustling crowd and a train of baggage, coming to meet the bridal party, escorted by his friends and kinsmen fully armed, to the sound of drums and instruments of music. Emerging from ambush, Yonasan attacked and cut them down; many fell, others made off into the hills, while the Jews took all their goods as spoil. The wedding was turned into mourning, and the sound of music to lamentation. Satisfied that the blood of their brother was fully avenged, Yonasan returned to the marshes of Jordan.

Bacchides heard this and came to the banks of Jordan on the Shabbos with a powerful force. Yonasan said to his men: 'Now is the time to fight for our lives; we are today in a worse situation than ever: the enemy in front, the waters of the Jordan behind, to right and left marsh and thicket; there is no escape. Cry to Heaven to save us from the hands of the enemy.' The battle started, and Yonasan had raised his hand to strike down Bacchides when he fell back and evaded him. Then Yonasan and his men leapt into the Jordan and swam over to the other side; but the enemy did not cross the river in pursuit. The army of Bacchides lost about a thousand men that day.

Bacchides returned to Yerushalayim and fortified a number of places in Judea with high walls, gates, and bars: the fortress at Jericho, Emmaus and Beit-Horon, Bethel, Timnath-Pharathon, and Tephon; in all of these he placed garrisons to harass Yisrael. He fortified the towns of Beit Tzur and Gaza and the citadel, placing forces and stores of provisions there. He took the sons of the leading men of the country as hostages and put them under guard in the citadel at Yerushalayim.

In the second month of the year 153, Alcimus gave orders to demolish the inner court of the Temple, thereby destroying the work of the prophets. But at the very moment when he began the demolition, Alcimus suffered a stroke, which put a stop to his activities. Paralyzed and with his speech impaired, he could not utter a word or give final instructions about his property. Thus he died in great torment. On learning that Alcimus was dead, Bacchides returned to the king, and for two years Judea had peace.

The renegades then conspired: 'Look!' they said, 'Yonasan and his people are living in peace and security. Let us bring Bacchides here; he will capture them all in a single night.' They went and conferred with Bacchides, and he set out with a large force, sending letters secretly to all his supporters in Judea, with instructions to seize Yonasan and his men. Fortunately the plan was discovered. About fifty of the ringleaders of this treachery in Judea were seized and put to death. Yonasan, Shimon, and their men then made their way out to Beit Basi in the desert, built up its ruined fortifications, and strengthened it. When Bacchides learned of this, he gathered together all his army and sent word to his renegade allies in Judea. He took up position against Beit

---

the year 153: 159 BCE

Basi, erecting siege engines, and attacked it for a long time. Yonasan left his brother Shimon in the town and slipped out into the country with a few men. He attacked Odomera and his people and the Phasirites in their encampment; he began to get the better of them and to advance towards Beit Basi with his forces.

Shimon and his men left the town and set fire to the siege engines. They fought Bacchides and defeated him. They applied a heavy pressure against him until his plan and his expedition proved fruitless, and he decided to return to his own country. They killed many of those at whose instigation Bacchides had invaded the land.

When Yonasan learned that Bacchides had left, he sent envoys to arrange terms of peace and a return of the Jewish prisoners. Bacchides agreed and did as Yonasan proposed, swearing to do him no harm for the rest of his life. He sent him back the prisoners he had previously taken from Judea and returned to his own country, never entering their territory again. Finally the war in Yisrael came to an end. Yonasan took up residence in Michmash and began to govern the people, rooting the godless out of Yisrael.

Chapter 10
Yonasan Rules the Nation

In the year 160 Alexander Epiphanes son of Antiochus came and took possession of Ptolemais, where he was welcomed and proclaimed king. When King Demetrius heard of this, he raised a huge army and marched out to

---

the year 160: 152 BCE

meet him in battle. At the same time Demetrius sent Yonasan a friendly and flattering letter, thinking to himself, 'Let us forestall Alexander by making peace with the Jews before Yonasan joins him against us, for he will remember all the harm we have done him by our treatment of his brothers and of his nation.' He gave Yonasan authority to collect and equip an army, conferred on him the title of ally, and ordered that the hostages in the citadel to be handed over to him. Yonasan came to Yerushalayim and read the letter aloud before all the people and the garrison of the citadel, who were filled with apprehension when they heard that the king had given Yonasan authority to raise an army. They surrendered the hostages to him, and he restored them to their families.

Yonasan moved his quarters to Yerushalayim and began to repair and rebuild the city. He gave orders to the workers to build the walls and surround Mount Zion with a fortification of squared stones. This was accomplished. The foreigners in the strongholds which Bacchides had built escaped, each man leaving his post and returning to his own country; however, in Beit Tzur some remained who had abandoned the law and ordinances, and who had found asylum there.

King Alexander heard of the promises which Demetrius had sent to Yonasan and was told of the battles and heroic deeds of Yonasan and his brothers, and the hardships they had endured. 'Where shall we ever find another man like this?' he exclaimed. 'Let us make him our friend and ally.' He therefore wrote a letter to Yonasan to this effect:

'King Alexander to his brother Yonasan, greeting.

'We have heard about you, what a valiant man you are and how fit you are to be our friend. Now, therefore, we appoint you this day to be High Priest of your nation with the title of King's Friend, to support our cause and to keep friendship with us.'

Alexander sent him a purple robe and a gold crown.

Yonasan assumed the vestments of the High Priest in the seventh month of the year 160 during the *Yom Tov* of Sukkos, at which time he gathered an army together and prepared a large supply of arms.

When this news reached Demetrius he was mortified. 'How did we come to let Alexander forestall us,' he asked, 'in gaining the friendship and support of the Jews? I too will send them cordial messages and offer honors and gifts to keep them on my side.' So he sent a message to the Jews to this effect:

> 'King Demetrius to the Jewish nation, greeting.
>
> 'We have heard with great pleasure that you have kept your agreements and remained in friendship with us and have not become allied with our enemies. Continue, then, to keep faith with us, and we shall reward you well for all that you do to support our cause, both by granting you numerous exemptions and making you gifts.
>
> 'I hereby release and exempt you and all Jews whatsoever from tribute, from the tax on salt, and from the crown taxes. From today and hereafter I release you from the one-third of the grain harvest and the half of the fruit harvest due to me. From today and for all time, I will no longer exact taxes from Judea or from the three administrative districts, formerly part of

---

the year 160: 152 BCE

Shomron and Galil, which I now attach to Judea. Jerusalem and its environs, with its tithes and tolls, shall be sacred and tax free. I also surrender authority over the citadel in Jerusalem and grant the High Priest the right to garrison it with men of his choice. All Jewish prisoners of war taken from Judea into any part of my kingdom, I release without ransom. No man shall exact any levy whatsoever on the cattle of the Jews. All their festivals, Shabbos, Rosh Chodesh, and appointed days, and three days preceding and following each festival, shall be days of exemption and release for all the Jews in my kingdom; no one shall have authority to impose any exaction or burden on a Jew in any respect.

'Jews shall be enlisted in the forces of the King to the number of thirty thousand men; they shall receive the usual army pay. Some of them shall be stationed in the great royal fortresses, others put in positions of trust in the kingdom. Their commanders and officers shall be of their own race, and they shall follow their own customs, just as the King has ordered for Judea.

'The three districts added to Judea from the territory of Shomron shall be attached to Judea so as to be under one authority, and subject to the High Priest alone.

'Ptolemais and the lands belonging to it I assign to the Temple in Jerusalem, to meet its necessary expenses. I give fifteen thousand silver shekels annually, charged on my own royal accounts, to be drawn from such places as may prove convenient. And the arrears of the subsidy, in so far as it has not been paid by the revenue officials, as it formerly was, shall henceforth be paid to provide for the needs of the Temple. In addition, the five thousand silver shekels which used to be taken from the annual income of the Temple are also released, because they belong to the ministering priests. Whoever shall take sanctuary in the Temple at Jerusalem, or in any part of its precincts, because of a debt to the crown or any other debt, shall be free from constraint on his person or on his property within my kingdom. The cost of the rebuilding and repair of the Temple shall be born by the royal revenue; also the repair of the walls of Jerusalem and its surrounding fortification, as well as of the fortresses in Judea, shall be at the expense of the royal revenue.'

When Yonasan and the people heard these proposals they did not believe or accept them, for they recalled the terrible calamity and harsh oppression Yisrael had suffered under the king. Therefore they favored Alexander, because it was he who had been the initiator of peaceful overtures, and so they remained his allies to the end.

King Alexander mustered powerful forces and took up his position against Demetrius, and the two kings engaged in battle. The army of Alexander fled, and Demetrius pursued and got the better of them. But although he fought hard till sunset, on that day Demetrius fell.

Then Alexander sent ambassadors to Ptolemy king of Egypt with the following message: 'I have returned to my kingdom and sit on the throne of my ancestors. I have assumed the government, defeated Demetrius, and made myself master of our country; for I gave him battle, and he and his army were crushed by us, and I sit on the throne of his kingdom. Let us now form an alliance; make me your son-in-law by giving me your daughter in marriage, and I will give presents to you and her worthy of your royal state.'

King Ptolemy replied: 'It was a happy day when you returned to the land of your ancestors and ascended the throne of their realm. I will now do as you ask; only come to Ptolemais so that we may meet, and I will become your father-in-law as you propose.'

In the year 162 Ptolemy set out from Egypt with his daughter Cleopatra, and arrived at Ptolemais, where King Alexander met him and Ptolemy gave him his daughter in marriage. The wedding was celebrated in royal style, with great pomp.

King Alexander wrote to Yonasan to come and meet him. Yonasan went in state to Ptolemais, where he met the two kings; he gave them silver and gold, and also made many gifts to their Friends; and so he won their favor.

There were some worthless Jewish renegades who conspired to lodge complaints against Yonasan. The king, however, paid no attention to them, but gave orders for Yonasan to exchange his garment for a robe of royal purple. The king had him sit at his side, and then ordered his officers to accompany Yonasan into the center of the city and proclaim that no one should bring any complaint against him or make trouble for him for any reason whatsoever. When this proclamation was made, and those who planned to lodge complaints saw Yonasan's splendor and the purple robe he wore, they ran away. Thus the king honored Yonasan, enrolling him in the first class of the order of King's Friends and making him a general and a provincial governor. Pleased with his success, Yonasan returned to Yerushalayim.

In the year 165 Demetrius, the son of King Demetrius, arrived in the land of his fathers from Crete. King Alexander was greatly upset by this news and returned to Antioch. Demetrius appointed as his commander Apollonius, the governor of Coele-Syria, who raised a powerful force and

---

the year 162: 150 BCE
the year 165: 147 BCE

encamped at Yavneh. From there he sent this message to Yonasan the High Priest: 'You alone resist us, and you are making me look ridiculous and absurd. Why do you defy us up there in the hills? If you have confidence in your forces, come down to meet us on the plain, and let us deal with each other there, for I have the power of cities behind me. Make inquiries; find out who I am and who are our allies; you will be told that you cannot stand your ground against us, for your predecessors have twice been routed in their own territory, and now you will not be able to resist my cavalry and such a force as mine, neither on the plain where there is not even a stone or a pebble to give you cover, or any place to which you can escape.'

Yonasan was provoked by this message from Apollonius. He took ten thousand men and marched from Yerushalayim, being joined by his brother Shimon with reinforcements. He laid siege to Yafo, whose gates the citizens had closed against him because Apollonius had a garrison there. But when fighting started the citizens were afraid and opened the gates; thus Yonasan became master of Yafo. When Apollonius heard he took three thousand cavalry and a large force of infantry, and marched to Ashdod intending to pass through it. At the same time, relying on his numerous cavalry, he advanced into the plain. Yonasan pursued him as far as Ashdod where the armies engaged in battle. But Apollonius had left a thousand cavalry in hiding in their rear, and Yonasan discovered that there was an ambush behind him. The enemy surrounded his army, showering arrows on our people from dawn till dusk. The soldiers stood fast as Yonasan had ordered them until the enemy cavalry grew weary. At that point Shimon led out his troops and joined battle with the enemy phalanx, now that the cavalry was exhausted. They were routed by him and fled.

The horsemen scattered across the plain and took refuge

in Ashdod, where they sought asylum in the temple of Dagon, their idol. But Yonasan set fire to Ashdod and its surrounding villages and plundered them; the temple of Dagon, and those who had taken refuge there, he destroyed with fire. The number of those who fell by the sword, together with those who lost their lives in the fire, reached eight thousand. Yonasan marched away from Ashdod, and encamped at Ashkelon, where the citizens came out to meet him with great pomp and ceremony. He and his men then returned to Yerushalayim loaded with spoil.

When King Alexander heard this, he further honored Yonasan, sending him the gold clasp which by custom is given to the King's Kinsmen. He also presented him with Ekron and all its districts.

Chapter 11

Ptolemy Intervenes

The king of Egypt collected a huge army, countless as the sand on the sea-shore, and a great fleet of ships, intending to make himself master of Alexander's kingdom by treachery and add it to his own. He set out for Syria with declarations of peace, and the people of the towns proceeded to open their gates to him and went to meet him; King Alexander had ordered them to do so because Ptolemy was his father-in-law.

As he progressed from town to town, Ptolemy left a detachment of troops in each of them as a garrison. When he reached Ashdod he was shown the burned-out temple of Dagon, the city itself and its ruined suburbs strewn with corpses, and, piled up along the way, the bodies of those who had been burned in the course of the fighting. They told the king that it was Yonasan's doing, hoping that he would reprimand him; but the king said nothing. Yonasan met him in state at Yafo, where they exchanged greetings and passed the night. Yonasan accompanied the king as far as the river Eleutherus and then returned to Yerushalayim. King Ptolemy made himself master of the coast towns as far as Seleucia-by-the-sea, all the time harboring malicious designs against Alexander.

He sent ambassadors to King Demetrius with the following message: 'I propose that you and I should make a pact: I will give you my daughter, now Alexander's wife, and you shall reign over the kingdom of your father. I now regret having given my daughter to him, for he has tried to kill me.'

He maligned Alexander in this way because he coveted his kingdom, and he took his daughter away and gave her to Demetrius. This led to a breach between him and Alexander, and to open enmity.

Ptolemy now entered Antioch, where he assumed the crown of Asia, becoming king of both Egypt and Asia.

King Alexander was at this time in Cilicia to put down the revolt of the inhabitants of that region. But when he heard the news he marched against Ptolemy, who met him with a powerful army and defeated him. Alexander fled to Arabia for protection and King Ptolemy was triumphant. Zabdiel, the Arab chieftain, cut off Alexander's head and sent it to Ptolemy. But two days later King Ptolemy died, and his garrisons in the fortresses were killed by the inhabitants. So in the year 167 Demetrius became king.

---

the year 167: 145 BCE

At this time Yonasan gathered the Judeans to assault the citadel in Yerushalayim, and they positioned many siege engines against it. But a number of renegades, enemies of their own people, went to the king and reported that Yonasan was besieging the citadel. The king was furious at the news and immediately moved his quarters to Ptolemais. He wrote to Yonasan ordering him to raise the siege, and to speedily meet him for a conference at Ptolemais.

When Yonasan received this letter, he gave orders for the siege to continue. Then, selecting the elder *chachamim* and *Cohanim* of Yisrael to accompany him, he embarked on his dangerous mission. He collected silver, gold, robes, and many other gifts, and went to meet King Demetrius at Ptolemais.

He won the favor of Demetrius, despite the attempt of some renegade Jews to lodge complaints against him. But the king treated him just as his predecessors had done, honoring him in the presence of all his Friends. He confirmed him in the high-priesthood, restored all his former honors, and appointed him head of the first class of the King's Friends.

Yonasan requested the king to exempt Judea, the three districts, and Shomron from tribute, promising him in return three hundred talents. King Demetrius consented, writing to Yonasan on all these affairs as follows:

'Greetings from King Demetrius to his brother Yonasan and to the Jewish nation:

'This is a copy of our letter written to our kinsman Lasthenes about you, which we have had made for your information:

"'Greetings from King Demetrius to his respected kinsman Lasthenes:

"'Because our friends the Jewish nation show us good will, and observe their obligations to us, we are resolved to become their benefactor. We have therefore settled on them the lands of Judea and the three districts of Apherema, Lydda, and Ramathaim, which are now transferred from Shomron to Judea, together with all the lands adjacent thereto, for the benefit of the priesthood at Jerusalem. This is a transfer of the annual dues which the King formerly received from these territories, from the produce of the soil and of the orchards. Other of our revenues, the tithes and tolls now pertaining to us, the salt-pans, and the crown taxes, all these we cede to them. These provisions are irrevocable from now for all future time. See to it then that you make a copy of them to be given to Yonasan and set by him in a conspicuous position on the holy mountain.'"

When King Demetrius saw that the country was quiet under his rule and resistance was at an end, he disbanded all his forces, sending every man home, with the exception of the foreign mercenaries he had hired from the islands of the Greeks. Then all the troops enlisted under his predecessors turned against the king. A certain Trypho, formerly of the party of Alexander, aware of the disaffection of all the forces towards Demetrius, went to Imalcue, the Arab chieftain, who had charge of the child Antiochus, Alexander's son, and kept pressing him to hand the boy over to him to be made king in succession to his father. He also informed

---

disbanded... sending... home: in modern language, he fired them—*i.e.* deprived them of their livelihood

with the exception: a further insult to all local troops

Imalcue of all the measures Demetrius was taking and of his unpopularity with his troops. He remained there for some time.

Meanwhile Yonasan sent a request to King Demetrius asking him to withdraw from the citadel in Yerushalayim and from the fortresses where the garrisons were constantly harassing Yisrael. [The King answered,] 'I will not only meet your request, but at the first opportunity I will bestow the highest honor upon you and your people. And now be so good as to send men to support me, for all my troops are in revolt.'

Yonasan dispatched three thousand fighting men to Antioch, and the king was much relieved at their arrival. The citizens were pouring into the center of the city, a hundred and twenty thousand strong, bent on killing the king. He took refuge in the palace while the citizens seized control of the streets and fighting broke out. King Demetrius called the Jews to help him, and they rallied to him at once. They then dispersed throughout the city and slaughtered that day as many as a hundred thousand, setting the city on fire and taking much booty. And thus they saved the king's life.

When the citizens saw that the Jews had the city completely at their mercy, their courage failed them and they clamored to the king to accept their surrender and to stop the Jews from fighting against them and destroying the city. They threw down their arms and made peace; and the Jews, now in high repute with the king and all his subjects, returned to Yerushalayim loaded with booty.

However, when King Demetrius was secure upon his throne, with the country subdued, he retracted all his promises and broke off relations with Yonasan; instead of repaying the benefits he had received, he put severe pressure upon him.

After this episode Trypho returned with the young Antiochus. When Antiochus was crowned, all the forces Demetrius had so contemptuously discharged rallied to the the new king. These fought against Demetrius, who was utterly defeated. Trypho brought up his elephants and made himself master of Antioch.

The young Antiochus wrote to Yonasan confirming him in the high-priesthood, with authority over the four districts, and making him one of the King's Friends. He also sent him a service of gold plate, and gave him the authority to drink from a gold cup, to be robed in purple, and to wear the gold clasp. He appointed Yonasan's brother Shimon as commanding officer of the area from the Ladder of Tzor to the borders of Egypt. Yonasan made a tour through the country on the far side of the river and the towns there, and all the forces of Syria gathered to his support.

Yonasan then went to Ashkelon, where he was received with great honor by the citizens. From there he went to Gaza, but the inhabitants closed the gates against him, so he blockaded the city, set fire to its suburbs, and plundered them. The citizens of Gaza then sought peace, and he made terms with them, taking the sons of their magistrates as hostages and sending them off to Yerushalayim. He himself continued his travels through the country in the direction of Damascus.

Yonasan heard that Demetrius's officers had arrived at Kadesh-HaGelili with a large force to prevent him from reaching his objective. He went to meet them, leaving his brother Shimon in Judea. Shimon took up a position against Beit Tzur and, after prolonged fighting, blockaded it. Finally the citizens sued for terms of peace, and Shimon consented;

he evicted them, took over the town, and installed a garrison there.

Yonasan, who had encamped with his army beside Lake Kinneret, marched out early in the morning into the plain of Asor. There in the plain the Greek army was advancing to meet him; they had set an ambush for him in the hills while they themselves confronted him. When the men from the ambush emerged and joined in the fighting, all Yonasan's men fled except Mattisyahu ben Avshalom and Yehudah ben Chalphi, officers in the army. Yonasan tore his clothes, put dust upon his head, and prayed. Then he turned upon the enemy and routed them into head-on flight. When the fugitives of Yonasan's army saw this reversal, they rallied to him and joined in the pursuit as far as the enemy base at Kadesh, where they encamped. That day about three thousand Greeks fell. Yonasan then returned in triumph to Yerushalayim.

Chapter 12
The Roman Treaty

Yonasan now saw his opportunity and sent selected men on a mission to Rome to confirm and renew the treaty of friendship with that city. He sent similar letters to Sparta and other places. The envoys traveled to Rome and went to the Senate House to deliver their message: 'Yonasan the High Priest and the Jewish people have sent us to renew their former pact of friendship and alliance.' The Romans gave them letters requiring the authorities in each place to give them safe conduct to Judea.

The following is a transcript of the letter which Yonasan wrote to the Spartans:

'Greetings to our brothers of Sparta from Yonasan the High Priest, the Senate of the Jews, the priests, and the rest of the Jewish people:

'On a previous occasion a letter was sent to Onias the High Priest from Arius your king, acknowledging our kinship; a copy is given below. Onias welcomed your envoy with full honors and received the letter in which the terms of the alliance and friendship were set forth. We do not regard ourselves as needing such alliances, since our support is the holy books in our possession. Nevertheless, we now venture to send and renew our pact of brotherhood and friendship with you, so that we may not become estranged, for it is many years since you wrote to us. We never lose any opportunity, on festal and other appropriate days, of remembering you at our sacrifices and in our prayers, as it is right and proper to remember kinsmen; and we rejoice at your fame. We ourselves have been under the pressure of hostile attacks on every side; all the surrounding kings have made war upon us. In the course of these wars we had no wish to trouble you or the rest of our allies and friends: we have the aid of Heaven to support us, and so we have been saved from our enemies and they have been humbled. Accordingly, we chose Numenius son of Antiochus and Antipater son of Jason, and have sent them to the Romans to renew our former friendship and alliance with them. We instructed them to go to you also with our greetings, and to deliver this letter about the renewal of our pact of brotherhood. And now we pray you to send us a reply to this letter.'

The following is a copy of the letter sent by the Spartans to Onias:

'Greetings to Onias the High Priest from Arius, King of Sparta:

'A document has been revealed which indicates that the Spartans and Jews are kinsmen, descended alike from Abraham. Now that we have learned this, we beg you to write and tell us how your affairs prosper. The message we return to you is, "What is yours, your cattle and every kind of property, is ours, and what is ours is yours," and we have therefore instructed our envoys to report this message.'

Meanwhile Yonasan heard that Demetrius's generals had returned to attack him with larger forces than before. He marched from Yerushalayim and met them in the region of Hamath, preventing them from entering his territory. He sent spies to their camp, who on their return reported that preparations were being made for a night attack. At sunset Yonasan gave orders to his men to stay awake all night, ready to arm themselves for battle; and he stationed outposts throughout the camp. When the enemy heard that Yonasan and his men were ready for battle, they were alarmed; their courage failed, and they withdrew, first lighting watch-fires in their camp. Yonasan and his men, seeing the watch-fires burning, did not realize what had happened until morning. Then Yonasan set out in pursuit, but failed to overtake them, for they had crossed the river Eleutherus. So Yonasan turned aside against the Arabs called Zabadaeans, and he dealt them a severe blow and plundered them. He struck camp and came to Damascus and then marched throughout the country.

Shimon set out and marched as far as Ashkelon and the neighboring fortresses. He then turned towards Yafo; he had heard that the citizens intended to hand it over to the supporters of Demetrius. Before they could do so, he occupied the town and placed a garrison there to defend it.

When Yonasan returned he convened the Sanhedrin. With their agreement he decided to build fortresses in Judea, to heighten the walls of Yerushalayim, and to erect a high barrier to separate the citadel from the city, in order to isolate it so that the garrison could neither buy nor sell. They assembled to rebuild the city, for the wall along the ravine to the east had partly collapsed. He repaired the section of the wall called Chaphenatha. Shimon also rebuilt and fortified Adida in the Shephelah, erecting gates and bars.

Trypho now aspired to be king of Asia, intending to rebel against King Antiochus and assume the crown himself. But he was afraid that Yonasan would fight to prevent this, so he searched for some means of capturing and killing him. He set off and reached Beit Shean. Yonasan marched out to meet him with forty thousand select troops, and he also reached Beit Shean. Seeing that Yonasan had a large force with him, Trypho was afraid to attack. Instead he received him honorably and commended him to all his Friends, gave him presents, and ordered his Friends and his troops to obey Yonasan as they would himself. He said to Yonasan: 'Why have you put all these men to so much trouble, when we are not at war? Send them home now and choose a few to accompany you, and come with me to Ptolemais. I will hand it over to you with all the other fortresses, the rest of the troops, and all the officials, and then I will leave the country. This is the only purpose of my coming.' Yonasan believed him and dismissed his forces, which returned to Judea. He retained three thousand men, two thousand of whom he left in the Galil while a thousand accompanied him. But when Yonasan entered Ptolemais, the citizens closed the gates, seized him, and killed all who had entered with him.

Trypho sent a force of infantry and cavalry into the Galil

---

so that the garrison...: he hoped thus to reduce them to starvation—the Citadel was still occupied by enemy troops

to the great plain, to wipe out all Yonasan's men. They now learned that Yonasan had been seized and was lost, along with his escort, but they encouraged each other and marched in close formation, ready for battle. When their pursuers saw they would fight to the death, they turned back. All came home safely to Judea, mourning for Yonasan and his followers and filled with alarm. All Yisrael was plunged in grief. The surrounding Greeks were now bent on destroying them root and branch, saying to themselves, 'The Jews have no leader or champion, so now is the time to attack, and we shall blot out all memory of them among men.'

Chapter 13

The High-Priesthood of Shimon

The news reached Shimon that Trypho had mustered a large force for the invasion and destruction of Judea, and the people were terrified. When Shimon saw this, he went up to Yerushalayim, called an assembly, and encouraged them with these words: 'I need not remind you of all that my brothers and I and my father's house have done for the Torah the holy Temple, the battles we have fought, and hardships we have endured. My brothers have all fallen in this cause, fighting for Yisrael, and I am the only one left. Now Heaven forbid that I should resist giving my own life in any moment of danger, for I am not worth more than my brothers. No! I will take up the cause of my nation and the *Beis HaMikdash*, of your wives and children, since all the Greeks in their hatred have gathered to destroy us.' With these words the courage of the people revived, and they answered by shouting: 'You shall be our leader in place of Yehudah and your brother Yonasan. Fight our battles, and we will do whatever you tell us.' So Shimon mustered all the fighting men and hurried to complete the walls of Yerushalayim until the city was fortified on all sides. He sent Yonasan ben Avshalom with a considerable force to Yafo, expelling its inhabitants and remaining in possession of the town.

Trypho marched out from Ptolemais with a large force to invade Judea, taking Yonasan with him as a prisoner. Shimon encamped at Adida on the edge of the plain. When Trypho leared that Shimon had come forward to replace his brother Yonasan, and that he was about to engage him in battle, he sent envoys to Shimon with the following message: 'We are detaining your brother Yonasan because of certain monies which he owed to the royal treasury in connection with the offices he held. To ensure that he will not again revolt if we release him, send one hundred talents of silver and two of his sons as hostages, and we will let him go.' Shimon realized that this was a trick, but he sent the money and the children to Trypho, fearing that otherwise he might arouse deep animosity among the people, who would say, 'It was because you did not send the money and the children that Yonasan lost his life.' So he sent the children and the hundred talents, but Trypho broke his word and did not release Yonasan.

After this, Trypho set out to invade the country and ravage it, taking a roundabout way through Adora. Shimon and his army marched parallel with him everywhere he went. Meanwhile the garrison of the citadel were sending emissaries to Trypho, urging him to come to them by way of the desert and to send them provisions. Trypho prepared to send all his cavalry, but that night there was a severe snowstorm, which prevented their arrival; so he withdrew into Gilead. When he reached Baskama he had Yonasan put to death, and there he was buried. Trypho then turned and went back to his own country.

Shimon had the body of his brother Yonasan brought to

Modi'in and buried in the town of their fathers; and all Yisrael cried and mourned him for many days. Shimon built a high monument over the tomb of his father and brothers, whose façade, front and back, was polished stone and which was visible from a great distance. He erected seven pyramids, for his father and mother and his four brothers, arranged in pairs. For the pyramids he contrived an elaborate design, surrounding them with great columns surmounted with trophies of armor to serve as a perpetual memorial, and between the trophies he placed carved ships, plainly visible to all at sea. This mausoleum, which he designed at Modi'in, stands to this day.

Trypho now plotted against the young King Antiochus and murdered him. He usurped his throne and assumed the crown of Asia. This was a disaster for the country.

Shimon rebuilt the fortresses of Judea, furnishing them with high towers and great walls with gates and bars, and gave them provisions. He sent representatives to King Demetrius to negotiate suspending taxes for the country, on the basis that all of Trypho's demands had been exorbitant. Demetrius replied favorably to this request and wrote him a letter in the following terms:

> 'Greetings from King Demetrius to Shimon the High Priest and friend of kings, and to the Senate and nation of the Jews:
>
> 'We have received the golden crown and the palm branch which you sent, and we are ready to make a lasting peace with you and to instruct the revenue officers to grant you immunities. All our agreements with

---

father and mother and... brothers: making six; presumably the seventh pyramid was for his own tomb

you stand, and the strongholds which you built shall remain yours. We give a free pardon for any errors of omission or commission, to take effect from the date of this letter. We remit the crown tax which you owed us, and every other tax formerly exacted in Jerusalem is henceforth cancelled. All those of you who are suitable for enrollment in our retinue shall be so enrolled. Let there be peace between us.'

In the year 170 Yisrael was released from the Greek tyranny. The people began to write on their contracts and agreements, 'In the first year of Shimon, the great High Priest, general and leader of the Jews.'

Shimon then invaded Gaza and surrounded it with his forces. He constructed a siege engine and brought it up to the town, made a breach in one of the towers, and captured it. The men on the siege engine leapt out of it into the town, and there was a great commotion. The townspeople and their wives and children climbed up on to the city wall with their garments torn, clamoring to Shimon to offer them terms. 'Do not treat us as our wickedness deserves,' they cried, 'but as your mercy prompts you.' Shimon came to terms with them and brought the war to an end. But he expelled them from the town, and after purifying the houses in which the idols had stood he made his entry with songs of thanksgiving and praise. He removed every pollution and settled men there who would keep the law. He strengthened its fortifications and built a residence in the city for himself.

The men in the citadel in Yerushalayim were prevented from going in and out to buy and sell in the country, so that famine set in and many of them died of starvation. They

---

the year 170: 142 BCE

pleaded with Shimon to accept their surrender, and he agreed, expelling them from the citadel and cleansing it from its pollutions. It was on the twenty-third day of the second month in the year 171 that he made his entry, with a chorus of praise and the waving of palm branches, with harps, cymbals, and zithers, with hymns and songs, to celebrate Yisrael's final elimination of a formidable enemy. Shimon decreed that this day should be observed as an annual festival. He fortified the *Har HaBayis* opposite the citadel, and he and his men took up residence there.

When Shimon realized that his son Yochanan had become a man, he made him commander of all the forces, with Gaza as his headquarters.

Chapter 14
Peace and Plenty

In the year 172 King Demetrius mustered his army and went into Media to recruit additional forces for his war against Trypho. When Arsakes, king of Persia and Media, heard that Demetrius had entered his territories, he sent one of his generals to capture him alive. The general marched out and defeated Demetrius, captured him and brought him to Arsakes, who put him in prison.

As long as Shimon lived Judea was at peace. He promoted his people's welfare, and they lived happily all

---

the year 171: 141 BCE
the year 172: 140 BCE
Arsakes: probably Artaxerxes

through the glorious days of his reign. Among other notable achievements, he captured the port of Yafo to secure his communications overseas. He extended his nation's territories and made himself master of the whole land. He repatriated a large number of prisoners of war. Without meeting any resistance he gained control over Gaza, Beit Tzur, and the Citadel, and removed their pollution.

The people farmed their land in peace, and the land produced its crops and the trees in the plains their fruit. Old men sat in the streets, talking together of their blessings; and the young men dressed themselves in splendid military style. Shimon supplied the towns with abundant food and equipped them with weapons for defence. His renown reached the ends of the earth. He restored peace to the land, and there were great rejoicings throughout Yisrael. Every man sat under his own vine and fig-tree, and men had no one to fear. Those were days when every enemy vanished from the land and every hostile king was crushed. Shimon gave his protection to the poor among the people; he observed the Torah faithfully and rid the country of lawless and wicked men. He gave new splendor to the Temple and furnished it with a wealth of sacred vessels.

The report of Yonasan's death reached Rome, and Sparta too, and they were deeply grieved. When they heard, however, that his brother Shimon had become High Priest in his place, and was in firm control of the country and all its towns, they inscribed on bronze tablets a renewal of the treaty of friendship and alliance which they had established with his brothers Yehudah and Yonasan. This was read before the assembly in Yerushalayim. The following is a copy of the letter from Sparta:

'Greetings from the rulers and city of Sparta to the High Priest Shimon, to the Senate, the priests, and the rest of the Jewish people, our brothers:

'The envoys you sent to our people have told us about your fame and honor, and their visit has given us great pleasure. We have entered a transcript of the message they brought in the minutes of the public assembly: "Numenius son of Antiochus and Antipater son of Jason, envoys of the Jews, visited us to renew their treaty of friendship with us. It was resolved by the public assembly to receive these men with honor and to place a copy of their address in the public archives, so that the Spartans might have it on permanent record. A copy of this document has been made for Shimon the High Priest."'

After this declaration, Shimon sent Numenius to Rome with a large gold shield, worth a thousand *maneh,* to confirm the alliance with the Romans.

When the people heard of these events they deliberated as to how they could express their gratitude to Shimon and his sons. For he, with his brothers and his father's family, had stood firm, fought off the enemies of Yisrael, and secured his nation's freedom. Accordingly, an inscription was engraved on tablets of bronze and placed on a monument on Mount Zion. A copy of the inscription follows:

'On the eighteenth day of the month of Elul, in the year 172, the third year of Shimon's high-priesthood, in "Asaramel"—a great assembly of priests, people, rulers of the nation, and elders of the land—the following facts were placed on record. Whereas our land had been subject to

---

the year 172: 140 BCE

Asaramel: probably a confused Greek form of עצרת עם, "a gathering of the people."

frequent wars, Shimon son of Mattisyahu, a priest of Yehoyariv's family, and his brothers, risked their lives in resisting the enemies of their people, in order that the *Mikdash* and the Torah might be preserved. They brought great glory to their nation. Yonasan rallied the nation, became their High Priest, and then was gathered to his fathers. Their enemies resolved to invade the land and destroy it, and to attack the *Beis HaMikdash*. Then Shimon came forward and fought for his nation. He spent large sums of his own money to arm the soldiers of his nation and to provide their pay. He fortified the towns of Judea, and Beit Tzur on the borders of Judea, formerly an enemy arsenal, and stationed a garrison of Jews there. He fortified Yafo by the sea, and Gaza near Ashdod, formerly occupied by the enemy. He settled Jews there and provided these towns with everything necessary for their welfare. When the people saw Shimon's patriotism and determination to win fame for his nation, they made him their leader and High Priest, in recognition of all that he had accomplished, of his just conduct, his loyalty to his nation, and his constant efforts to enhance its renown. His leadership was crowned with success, and the Greeks were expelled from the land, as were the troops in Yerushalayim who had built themselves a citadel in the city of David, from which they freely defiled the whole precinct of the *Mikdash* and violated its purity. Shimon settled Jews there and fortified it for the security of the land and of the city, and he raised the height of the walls of Yerushalayim. King Demetrius confirmed him in the office of High Priest, made him one of his Friends, and granted him the highest honors; for he had heard that the Romans were declaring the Jews their friends, allies, and brothers, and had gone in state to meet Shimon's envoys.

'The Jews and their priests have confirmed Shimon as their leader and High Priest in perpetuity, until a true prophet should appear. He is to be their general, and to have full charge of the *Beis HaMikdash*; in addition he is assigned to supervise their labor, the work throughout the country, and all arms and fortifications are entrusted to him. He is to be obeyed by all; all contracts in the country are to be drawn up in his name. He is to wear the purple robe and the gold clasp.

'None of the people or the priests shall have authority to abrogate any of these decrees, to oppose commands issued by Shimon, or convene any assembly in the land without his consent, to be robed in purple, or to wear the gold clasp. Whoever shall contravene these provisions, or neglect any of them, shall be liable to punishment. The people have unanimously decided that Shimon shall officiate in the ways here enumerated. Shimon has agreed and consented to be High Priest, general and ethnarch over both [ordinary] Jews and priests, and to be the *parnas* of them all.'

This inscription, it was declared, should be engraved on bronze tablets and set up within the precincts of the *Mikdash* in a conspicuous position, and copies should be placed in the treasury and in the keeping of Shimon and his sons.

Chapter 15
The Last Battle

Antiochus son of King Demetrius sent a letter from overseas to Shimon, the High Priest and ethnarch of the Jews, and to the whole nation. The contents were as follows:

---

ethnarch: Greek, "ruler of the people."
over Jews and priests: i.e., over Cohen, Levi, and Yisrael

'Greetings from King Antiochus to Shimon, High Priest and Ethnarch, and to the Jewish nation:

'Whereas certain traitors have seized my ancestral kingdom, I have now decided to assert my claim to it, so that I may restore it to its former condition. I have raised a large body of mercenaries and fitted out ships of war. I intend to land in my country and to attack those who have ravaged my kingdom and destroyed many of its cities. Now therefore I confirm all the tax remissions which my royal predecessors granted you, and all their other remissions of tribute. I permit you to mint your own coinage as currency for your country. Jerusalem and the Temple shall be free. All the arms you have prepared, and the fortifications which you have built and now hold, shall remain yours. All debts now owing to the royal treasury and all future liabilities thereto shall be cancelled from this time on and forever. When we have re-established our kingdom, we shall confer the highest honors upon you, your nation and Temple, to make your country's greatness apparent to the whole world.'

In the year 174 Antiochus marched into his ancestral domain, and all the armed forces came over to him, leaving very few with Trypho. Antiochus pursued him, and Trypho came as a fugitive to Dor by the sea. He knew that his position was desperate now that all his troops had deserted. Antiochus, at the head of a hundred and twenty thousand trained soldiers and eight thousand horsemen, laid siege to Dor. He encircled the town and his ships joined in the blockade from the sea. He thus exerted heavy pressure on it from both land and sea, and prevented anyone from leaving or entering.

---

the year 174: 138 BCE

Numenius and his party arrived from Rome with a letter to the various kings and countries, which read as follows:

'Greetings from Lucius, Consul of the Romans, to King Ptolemy:

'Envoys have come to us from our friends and allies the Jews, sent by Shimon the High Priest and the Jewish people, to renew their original treaty of friendship and alliance. They brought a gold shield worth a thousand *minas*. We have decided, therefore, to write to the kings and countries, requiring them to do no harm to the Jews, nor make war on them or their cities or their country, nor ally themselves with those who so make war. And we have decided to accept the shield from them. If, therefore, any traitors have escaped from their country to you, hand them over to Shimon the High Priest to be punished by him according to the law of the Jews.'

The same message was sent to King Demetrius, to Attalus, Ariarathes, Arsakes, Sampsakes, and the Spartans, and also to the following places: Delos, Myndos, Sicyon, Caria, Samos, Pamphylia, Lycia, Halicarnassus, Rhodes, Phaselis, Cos, Side, Aradus, Gortyna, Cnidus, Cyprus, and Cyrene. A copy was sent to Shimon the High Priest.

King Antiochus laid siege to Dor for the second time, and launched repeated attacks against it; he had siege engines constructed, and blockaded Trypho, preventing all movement in or out of the town.

---

for the second time: some manuscripts read "on the second day." The phrase "for the second time" might simply mean "again and again" or "persistently."

Shimon sent Antiochus two thousand picked men to assist him, with silver and gold and much equipment, but he refused the offer. He repudiated all his previous agreements with Shimon and broke off relations. He sent Athenobius, one of the Friends, to parley with him. This was his message: 'You are occupying Jaffa and Gaza and the citadel in Jerusalem, cities that belong to my kingdom. You have destroyed their territories and done great damage to the country, and asserted your authority over many places in my kingdom. I demand the return of the cities you have captured, and the surrender of the tribute exacted from places beyond the frontiers of Judea over which you have assumed control. Otherwise you must pay five hundred talents of silver on their account, and another five hundred as compensation for the destruction you have caused and for the loss of tribute from the cities. Failing this, we shall go to war with you.'

Athenobius, the King's Friend, came to Yerushalayim, and when he saw the splendor of Shimon's establishment, the gold and silver vessels on his sideboard, and his display of wealth, he was amazed. He delivered the king's message, to which Shimon replied: 'We have not occupied other people's land or taken other people's property, but only the inheritance of our ancestors, unjustly seized for a time by our enemies. We have grasped our opportunity and have claimed our patrimony. With regard to Yafo and Gaza, which you demand, these towns were doing a great deal of damage among our people and in our land. For these we offer one hundred talents.'

Athenobius answered not a word, but went off in a rage to the king; he reported what Shimon had said, and described Shimon's splendor and all the things he had seen. The king was furious.

Meanwhile Trypho boarded a ship and made good his escape to Orthosia. The king appointed Kendebaeus as commander-in-chief of the coastal zone, and gave him infantry and cavalry. He instructed him to blockade Judea, to rebuild Kidron and strengthen its gates, and to make war on our people, while he himself continued the pursuit of Trypho. Kendebaeus arrived in Yavneh and began to harass our people by invading Judea, and by capturing and killing the inhabitants. He rebuilt Kidron, stationing cavalry and troops there to patrol the roads of Judea, in accordance with the king's instructions.

Yochanan came from Gaza and reported to his father Shimon the results of Kendebaeus's campaign. Shimon summoned his two eldest sons, Yehudah and Yochanan, and said to them: 'My brothers and I and my father's family have fought Yisrael's battles from our youth until this day, and often we have been successful in rescuing Yisrael. Now I am old, but mercifully you are in the prime of life. Take my place and my brother's and go out and fight for our nation. And may help from on high be with you.'

He then levied from the country twenty thousand select warriors and cavalry, and they marched against Kendebaeus. After passing the night at Modi'in they rose early and proceeded to the plain, where a large force of infantry and cavalry stood ready to meet them on the far side of a gully. When his army had taken up the opposite position, Yochanan saw that his men were afraid to cross the gully. So he crossed first by himself, and when his men saw him they followed. Yochanan drew up his army with the cavalry in the center of the infantry, for the enemy cavalry were very numerous. The trumpets were sounded, and Kendebaeus and his army were routed; many of them fell, and the remainder took refuge in the fortress. It was in this engagement that Yochanan's brother Yehudah was wounded.

Yochanan kept up the pursuit until Kendebaeus reached Kidron, which he had rebuilt. The enemy took refuge in the towers in the open country around Ashdod, whereupon Yochanan set fire to Ashdod. Some two thousand of the enemy fell in the fighting, and Yochanan returned to Judea in safety.

Meanwhile Ptolemaeus son of Abubus had been appointed commander for the plain of Yericho. He had great wealth, for he was the High Priest's son-in-law. But he became over-ambitious; he proposed to make himself master of the country and plotted to put Shimon and his sons out of the way. In the course of a tour to inspect the towns in that region and to attend to their needs, Shimon came to Yericho with his sons Mattisyahu and Yehudah in the year 177, in the eleventh month, the month of Shevat. The treacherous son of Abubus received them at Dok, the small fort he had built, and entertained them lavishly. But he had men in concealment there, and when Shimon and his sons had drunk freely, Ptolemaeus and his accomplices jumped up, seized their weapons, and rushed in to the banquet. They attacked Shimon and killed him, along with his two sons and some of his servants. It was an act of base treachery in which evil was returned for good.

Ptolemaeus sent news of this in a dispatch to the king, asking him to send troops to his assistance and to give him authority over the country and its towns. He sent some of his men to Gaza to kill Yochanan, and wrote to the army officers urging them to join him, and offering them silver, gold and presents. Other troops he sent to take Yerushalayim and *Har HaBayis*. But someone ran ahead and reported to Yochanan at Gaza that his father and brothers had been

---

the year 177: 134 BCE

murdered, and that Ptolemaeus had sent men to kill him as well. When Yochanan heard this he was beside himself; he arrested the men who came to kill him, and put them to death because he had discovered their plot against his life.

The rest of the story of Yochanan, his wars and the deeds of valor he performed, the walls he built, and his exploits, are written in the annals of his high-priesthood from the time when he succeeded his father.

THE SECOND BOOK OF THE MACCABEES

Foreword:

Letters to the Jews in Egypt

'To our Jewish kinsmen in Egypt—the Jews who are in Jerusalem and those who are in the country of Judea send you our brotherly greeting:

'May God give you peace and prosperity and remember His covenant with Abraham, Isaac, and Jacob, His faithful servants. May He give to you all a will to fear Him, to fulfill His purposes eagerly with heart and soul. May He give you a mind open to his Torah and mitzvos. May He make peace for you and answer your prayers, and be reconciled to you and not forsake you in a difficult time. Here and now we are praying for you.

'In the reign of Demetrius, in the year 169, we Jews wrote to you. It was during the persecution and the crisis that came upon us in those years, since the time when Jason and his partisans revolted from the holy land and the kingdom. They set the *azarah* of the *Beis HaMikdash* on fire and shed innocent blood. Then we prayed to God and were answered. We offered a *kor-*

---

the year 169: 143 BCE
azarah: the courtyard

ban minchah of fine flour, we lit the *Menorah,* and we set out the *Lechem HaPanim.* And now, you are to observe the celebration of a '*Yom Tov* of Sukkos' in the month of Kislev.'

Written in the year 188.

'From the people of Jerusalem and Judea, from the Sanhedrin, and from Yehudah, to Aristobulus, the teacher of King Ptolemy and a member of the high-priestly family, and to the Jews in Egypt: greeting and good health.

'We have been saved by God from great dangers, and give Him thanks, as men standing ready to resist the king. It was God who drove out the enemy force from the holy city.

'When the king entered Persia with an army that seemed invincible, they were cut to pieces in the temple of Nanaea through a stratagem employed by Nanaea's priests. Antiochus, along with his companions, arrived at the temple to marry the goddess, in order to secure the considerable treasure by way of dowry. After the priests made the preparations, Antiochus entered the temple precinct with a small retinue. When Antiochus entered, the priests shut the sanctuary, opened a secret door in the paneling, and hurled stones at them. The king fell, as if struck by a thunderbolt. They hacked off limbs and heads and threw them to those outside. Blessed in all things be our God, who handed over the evil-doers to death!

'We are about to celebrate the purification of the

---

korban minchah: a flour-sacrifice

the year 188: 124 BCE

temple on the twenty-fifth of Kislev, and think it right to inform you, so that you also may celebrate a "*Yom Tov* of Sukkos," in honor of the fire which appeared when Nechemiah offered sacrifices, after he had built the *Mikdash* and the altar. When our fathers were carried off to Persia, the pious *cohanim* of those days secretly took fire from the altar and concealed it in a dry well. It proved a safe hiding-place and remained undiscovered. After many years had passed, in Hashem's good time, Nechemiah was sent back by the king of Persia. He then sent descendants of the *cohanim* who had hidden it to retrieve the fire, and they informed our people that they found, not fire, but a thick liquid. Nechemiah ordered them to draw some out and bring it to him. When the *korban* had been presented, he ordered the *cohanim* to sprinkle this liquid over the wood and the limbs laid upon it, which they did. After some time the sun, which earlier had been hidden by clouds, shone out, and the altar burst into a great blaze, so that everyone marveled! As the sacrifice was burning, the *cohanim* and all those who witnessed this awesome phenomenon offered a prayer, led by Nechemiah.

'The following prayer was recited: "O Lord God, Creator of all things, the terrible, the great, the just, and the merciful, the only King, the only gracious one, the only giver, the only just, omnipotent, and everlasting one, who delivers Yisrael from every evil, who chose the patriarchs and set them apart: accept this sacrifice on behalf of Your whole people Yisrael. They are Your own—watch over them and sanctify them. Gather the dispersed, free those who are slaves among the heathen, look favorably on the despised and detested; let the heathen know that You are our God. Punish our oppressors for their insolent brutality and make them suffer torment; but plant Your people in Your place, as Moses said."

'Then the *Levi'im* sang the *mizmorim*. After the limbs of the *korban* had been consumed, Nechemiah further ordered that great stones should enclose what remained of the liquid. At this a flame shot up, but hardly had the light been reflected from the altar when it burnt itself out.

'These events became widely known. The king of Persia was told that in the place where the priests who were deported had hidden the fire, a liquid had appeared, and that Nechemiah and his companions had used it to burn up the limbs of a sacrifice. When he had verified the fact, the king enclosed the site and made it sacred. The custodians he appointed received a share of the very substantial revenue that the king derived from it. Nechemiah and his companions called the liquid "nephthar," which means "purification"; but most people call it "naphtha."'

Chapter One
Exile and Return

The records show that it was the prophet Yirmiyah who ordered the exiles to hide the fire, as has been mentioned; also that, having passed on the Torah to them, he charged them not to neglect the ordinances of the Lord, or be led astray by the sight of images of gold and silver with all their finery. In similar words he appealed to them not to abandon the Torah.

Further, this document records that prompted by a divine message, the prophet gave orders that the *Mishkan* and the *Aron* should go with him. Then he departed to the mountain from the top of which God showed Moshe the promised land. When he reached the mountain, Yirmiyah found a cave-dwelling; he carried the tent, the *Aron*, and the *ketores*-altar into it, then blocked up the entrance. Some of his companions tried to determine the way there, but were unable to find it. When Yirmiyah learned of this he reprimanded them. 'The place shall remain unknown ,' he said, 'until God finally gathers His people together and shows mercy to them. Then the Lord will reveal these things, and the glory of the Lord will appear in a cloud, as it was seen both in the time of Moshe and when Shlomoh prayed that the *Mikdash* might receive *kedushah* according to its worth.'

It was also related that Shlomoh, having the gift of wisdom, offered a *korban* of dedication at the completion of the *Mikdash;* and that, just as Moshe prayed to God and fire descended from heaven and burnt up the *korbanos,* so Shlomoh prayed and the fire came down and consumed the *korban olah.* (Moshe said: 'The *chattas* was burned up in the same way because it was not eaten.') Shlomoh celebrated the feast for eight days.

These same facts are stated in the official records and in the memoirs of Nechemiah. Just as Nechemiah collected the chronicles of the kings, the writings of the prophets, the words of David, and royal letters about *korbanos,* to establish his library, so Yehudah also has collected all the books that had been scattered as a result of our recent conflict. These are in our possession, and if you need any, send messengers for them.

So, since we are about to celebrate the purification of the *Mikdash,* we are writing to impress upon you the duty of celebrating this festival. God has saved His whole people and granted to all of us the Holy Land, the kingship, the priesthood, and the consecration, as He promised by the law; and we have confidence in Him that He will soon be merciful to us and gather us from every part of the world to the *Beis HaMikdash*. For He has delivered us from great evils and purified the Temple.

Chapter Two
A Preface to This Abridgement

In the five books of Jason of Cyrene, he has set out the history of Yehudah Maccabee and his brothers, the purification of the great *Beis HaMikdash*, and the dedication of the altar. He has described the battles with Antiochus Epiphanes and with his son Eupator, and the apparitions from heaven which appeared to those who vied with one another in fighting zealously for Judaism. Few though they were, they ravaged the whole country and routed the foreign hordes; they restored the world-renowned Temple, freed the city of Yerushalayim, and reaffirmed the laws which were in danger of being abolished. All this they achieved because the Lord was merciful and gracious to them.

I shall try to summarize these five books of Jason in a single work; for I was struck by the mass of statistics and the difficulty which the bulk of the material causes to those wishing to grasp the narratives of this history. I have tried to provide for the entertainment of those who read for pleasure, the convenience of students who must commit the facts to memory, and the profit of even the casual reader. The task which I have taken upon myself in making this summary is not easy. It requires hard work and late nights, just as it is no light task for the man who plans a dinner-party and aims to satisfy his guests. Nevertheless, I will gladly undergo this hard labor for the benefit of readers in general.

---

for the benefit of: other manuscripts read "to win the gratitude of..."

I will leave to the original author the minute discussion of every detail, and concentrate on the main points of my outline. As the architect of a new house must concern himself with the whole of the structure, while the man who paints frescoes on the walls needs to discover only what is necessary for the ornamentation, so, I judge, it is with me also. It is the province of the original author of a history to claim the subject, not only providing a broad perspective but inquiring closely into particular details and questions. The writer whose intent is to paraphrase, in order to clarify, must be allowed to compromise a full treatment of the subject matter for the sake of providing the reader with a concise and clear expression of the text.

Here, then, without adding anything further, I begin my narrative. It would be absurd to make a lengthy introduction to the history and cut short the history itself.

Chapter Three
Syrian Oppression

During the rule of the High Priest Onias, the Holy City enjoyed complete peace and prosperity, and the laws were still observed most scrupulously because he was a pious man and hated wickedness. The kings themselves held the sanctuary in honor and used to embellish the Temple with the most splendid gifts; even Seleucus, king of Asia, bore all the expenses of the sacrificial worship from his own revenues.

But a certain Shimon, of the clan of Bilgah, who had

Bilgah: other manuscripts read "Benjamin"

been appointed *gabbai* of the *Beis HaMikdash,* quarreled with the High Priest about the regulation of the city market. Unable to get the better of Onias, he went to Apollonius son of Thrasaeus, then governor of Coele-Syria and Phoenicia, and alleged that the treasury at Yerushalayim was full of untold riches—indeed the total of the accumulated amount was incalculable. Nor did it correspond with the account for the sacrifices! He suggested that these deposits might be brought under the control of the king. When Apollonius met the king, he reported what he had been told about the riches. The king selected Heliodorus, his chief minister, and sent him with orders to remove these treasures.

Heliodorus set off at once, ostensibly to make a tour of inspection of the cities of Coele-Syria and Phoenicia, but in fact to carry out the purpose of the king. When he arrived at Yerushalayim and had been courteously received by the High Priest and the citizens, he explained his mission concerning the allegations and asked if they were in fact true. The High Priest explained that the deposits were held in trust for widows and orphans, apart from what belonged to Hyrcanus son of Tobias, a man of very high standing. He told Heliodorus that the matter was being misrepresented by the impious Shimon. In all there were four hundred talents of silver and two hundred of gold. It was unthinkable, he said, that those who had relied on the sanctity of the place, on the dignity and inviolability of the world-famous Temple, should suffer such an injustice. But Heliodorus, by virtue of the king's orders, replied that these deposits must without question be handed over to the royal treasury.

He fixed a day and went into the temple to make an

Appolonius son of Thrasaeus: later in the text he is referred to as "son of Menestheus"

inventory, resulting in great distress throughout the whole city. The priests, prostrating themselves in their vestments before the altar, prayed to Heaven, to the Divine Lawgiver who had made deposits sacred, to keep them intact for their rightful owners. The High Priest's expression pierced every heart, for his face betrayed the anguish of his soul. His body shook with fear, and the pain he felt was clearly apparent to the onlookers. The people rushed pell-mell from their houses to join together in supplication because of the dishonor which threatened the *Beis HaMikdash*. Women in sackcloth, their breasts bare, filled the streets; unmarried girls who kept themselves secluded ran to the gates or walls of their houses, while others leaned out from the windows, all with their arms outstretched appealing for help from Heaven. It was pitiful to see the crowd all lying prostrate in utter confusion, and to witness the High Priest in an agony of apprehension.

While the people were calling upon the Lord Almighty to keep the deposits intact and safe for those who had deposited them, Heliodorus proceeded to carry out his decision. But at the very moment when he arrived with his bodyguard at the treasury, the Ruler of spirits and of all powers produced a mighty apparition, so that all who had had the audacity to accompany Heliodorus were faint with terror, stricken with panic at the power of God. They saw a horse, splendidly caparisoned, with a rider of terrible aspect wearing golden armor; it rushed fiercely at Heliodorus and, rearing up, attacked him with its hooves. The rider was wearing golden armor. There also appeared to Heliodorus two young men of surpassing strength and glorious beauty, splendidly dressed. They stood on either side of him and scourged him, raining ceaseless blows upon him. He fell suddenly to the ground, overwhelmed by a great darkness, and his men snatched him up and put him on a litter. This man, who so recently had entered the treasury with a great throng and his whole bodyguard, was now carried off by them quite helpless, publicly compelled to acknowledge the sovereignty of God.

While he lay speechless, deprived by this Divine act of all hope of recovery, the Jews were praising God for the miracle he had performed in His house. The atmosphere in the Temple, which a short time before was tense with alarm and confusion, was now a scene of great joy and festivity because God had appeared.

Some of Heliodorus' companions hastily begged Onias to pray to the Most High to spare the life of their master, now breathing his very last gasp. The High Priest, fearing that the king might suspect that Heliodorus had met with foul play at the hands of the Jews, brought a *korban* for the man's recovery. As he was making the *kapparah,* the same young men, dressed as before, again appeared to Heliodorus. They stood over him and said: 'Be very grateful to Onias the High Priest; for his sake God has spared your life. You have been scourged by God; now tell all men of his mighty power.' When they had said this, they vanished.

Heliodorus offered a sacrifice and made lavish vows to the Lord who had spared his life; then, after taking friendly leave of Onias, he led his troops back to the king. He bore witness to everyone of the miracles of the supreme God which he had seen with his own eyes.

When the king asked him what sort of man would be suitable to send to Yerushalayim another time, Heliodorus replied: 'If you have an enemy or someone plotting against your government, that is the place to send him; you will receive him back soundly flogged, if he survives at all, for beyond doubt there is a Divine power surrounding the Temple. He whose habitation is in heaven watches over it Himself and gives it His aid; those who approach the place with evil intent He strikes and destroys.'

So this is the story of Heliodorus and the preservation of the treasury.

Chapter Four
Treachery

But what about Shimon, mentioned earlier, the man who had made allegations against his country's finances, who had slandered Onias, alleging that he had attacked Heliodorus and had been the author of these troubles? He had the nerve to accuse Onias of conspiracy against the government—this benefactor of the holy city, this protector of his fellow-Jews, this zealot for the Torah! The enmity became so intense that one of Simon's trusted followers even resorted to murder.

Onias, realizing that Simon's rivalry was dangerous and that Apollonius son of Menestheus, governor of Coele-Syria and Phoenicia, was encouraging his evil ways, paid a visit to the king. He did not appear as an accuser of his fellow-citizens, but as one who was concerned for the interests of all the Jews, both as a nation and as individuals. For he saw that unless the king intervened there could not possibly be peace in public affairs, nor could Shimon be stopped in his mad pursuit of power.

But when Seleucus was dead and had been succeeded by Antiochus, known as Epiphanes, then Jason, Onias's brother, obtained the high-priesthood by corrupt means. He petitioned the king and promised him three hundred and sixty talents in silver coin immediately, and eighty talents from future revenue. In addition he obligated himself to pay another hundred and fifty talents for the authority to institute a sports-stadium, to arrange for the education of young men there, and to enroll in Yerushalayim a group to be known as the 'Antiochenes'. The king agreed, and, as soon as he had seized the high-priesthood, Jason made the Jews conform to the Greek way of life.

He set aside the royal privileges established for the Jews through the agency of John, the father of that Eupolemus who negotiated a treaty of friendship and alliance with the Romans. He forbade the Torah way of life and introduced practices which were against the law. He lost no time in establishing a sports-stadium at the foot of the citadel itself, and he enlisted the most outstanding of the young men, designating them as athletes worthy of wearing the Greek athlete's hat.

Hellenism reached a high point with the introduction of foreign customs through the boundless wickedness of the impious Jason, who was a High Priest in name only. As a result, the priests no longer had any enthusiasm for their duties at the altar, but despised the Temple and neglected the sacrifices; and, in defiance of the law, they eagerly contributed to the expenses of the wrestling-school whenever the opening gong summoned them. They placed no value on their hereditary duties, but cared above everything for Hellenic honors. Because of this disdain for their sacred office, they would suffer terrible misfortunes, and the very men whose way of life they strove after, and tried so hard to imitate, would become their vindictive enemies.

When the quinquennial games were being held at Tyre in the presence of the king, the blackguard Jason sent, as envoys to represent Yerushalayim, several Antiochenes carrying three hundred drachmas in cash for the sacrifice to Hercules. Even the bearers thought it improper that this money should be used for a sacrifice, and considered that it should be spent otherwise. So, thanks to the bearers, the money designated by the sender for the sacrifice to Hercules went to fit out the triremes.

When Appolonius son of Menestheus was sent to Egypt to crown King Philometor, Antiochus learnt that Philometor was now hostile to his state, and became anxious for his own security. So he went to Yafo, and then on to Yerushalayim, where he was lavishly welcomed by Jason and the city and received with torch-light and ovations. After this, he quartered his army in Phoenicia.

Three years later Jason sent Menelaus, brother of the Shimon mentioned above, to convey money to the king and to carry out his directions about urgent business. But Menelaus established his position with the king by acting as if he were a person of great authority, outbid Jason by three hundred talents in silver, and so diverted the high-priesthood to himself. He arrived back with the royal mandate, but with nothing else to make him worthy of the high-priesthood; he still had the temper of a cruel tyrant and the fury of a savage beast. Jason, who had supplanted his own brother, was now supplanted in his turn and forced to flee to Ammonite territory. As for Menelaus, he continued to hold the high-priesthood but without ever paying any of the money he had promised the king, although it was demanded by Sostratus, the commander of the citadel, who was responsible for collecting the revenues. Consequently, they were both summoned by the king. As their deputies, Menelaus left his brother Lysimachus, and Sostratus left Crates, the commander of the Cypriots.

It was at this point that the inhabitants of Tarsus and

---

triremes: a kind of war-ship with three ranks of oars

Mallus revolted because their cities had been handed over as a gift to the king's concubine Antiochis. The king hastened off to restore order, leaving as regent Andronicus, one of his ministers. Menelaus, thinking he had obtained a favorable opportunity, made a present to Andronicus of some of the gold plate belonging to the *Beis HaMikdash,* which he had appropriated. He had already sold some of it to Tzor and to the neighboring cities. When Onias heard this on good authority, he withdrew to safety at Daphne near Antioch and denounced him. As a result, Menelaus approached Andronicus privately and urged him to kill Onias. The regent went to Onias bent on treachery; he greeted him, gave him assurances on oath, and persuaded him, though still suspicious, to leave his sanctuary. Then at once, with no respect for justice, he killed him.

Onias' murder angered and alarmed not only Jews, but many from other nations as well. So when the king returned from Cilicia, the Jews of Antioch sent him a petition about the senseless killing, indicating that the gentiles shared their detestation of the crime. Antiochus was deeply grieved, and was moved to pity and tears as he thought of the prudence, integrity and disciplined habits of the dead man. In a burning fury, he immediately stripped Andronicus of the purple, tore off his clothes, led him round the whole city to that very place where he had committed sacrilege against Onias, and there disposed of the murderer. Thus the Lord repaid him with the retribution he deserved.

Lysimachus committed many acts of sacrilegious plunder in Yerushalayim with the connivance of Menelaus. When the news of their actions became public and the people heard that much of the gold plate had been disposed of, they banded together against Lysimachus. Since the crowds were seething with rage and getting out of hand, Lysimachus armed some three thousand men and launched a vicious attack, led by a certain Auranus, a man advanced in years and as foolish as he was old. Realizing that the attack came from Lysimachus, some of the crowd seized stones and others staves of wood, while others again took handfuls of the ashes that were available, and there was complete confusion as they all hurled them at Lysimachus and his men. As a result, they wounded many, killed some, and routed them all; the sacrilegious man himself they dispatched near the treasury.

An action was brought against Menelaus in connection with this incident. When the king came to Tyre, three men sent by the Sanhedrin pleaded the case before him. Menelaus's cause was as good as lost, but he promised a large sum of money to Ptolemaeus son of Dorymenes to persuade the king. So Ptolemaeus led the king aside into a colonnade, as if to get some air, and convinced him to change his mind. The king acquitted Menelaus, the cause of all the mischief, dismissed the charges brought against him, and condemned his unfortunate accusers to death, men who would have been discharged as entirely innocent had they appeared even before Scythians. Ironically, those who had pleaded for their city, their people, and their sacred vessels, suffered the unjust penalty. Responding to this tragic turn of events, even some of the Tyrians showed their detestation of the crime by providing a splendid funeral for the victims. Menelaus, thanks to the greed of those in power, remained in office. He went from bad to worse, this arch-plotter against his own fellow-citizens.

Chapter Five
Surprise Attack

About this time Antiochus undertook his second invasion

of Egypt. Apparitions were seen in the sky all over Yerushalayim for nearly forty days: galloping horsemen in golden armor, companies of spearmen standing to arms with swords unsheathed, and cavalry divisions in battle order. Charges and countercharges were made on each side, shields were shaken, spears massed and javelins hurled; breastplates and golden ornaments of every kind shone brightly. All men prayed that this apparition might portend good.

Upon a false report of Antiochus's death, Jason collected no less than a thousand men and made a surprise attack on Yerushalayim. The defenders on the wall were driven back and the city was finally taken; Menelaus took refuge in the citadel, and Jason continued to massacre his fellow-citizens without pity. He did not realize that success against one's own kindred is the greatest of failures, and he imagined that the trophies he raised marked the defeat of enemies, not of fellow-countrymen. He did not, however, gain control of the government; he gained only dishonor as the result of his plot, and returned again as a fugitive to Ammonite territory. His career came to a miserable end: after being imprisoned by Aretas, the ruler of the Arabs, he fled from city to city, hunted by all. He was hated as a rebel against the Torah, detested as the executioner of his country and his fellow-citizens, and finally was driven to take refuge in Egypt. In the end the man who had banished so many from their native land himself died in exile after setting sail for Sparta, where he had hoped to obtain shelter because of the Spartans' kinship with the Jews. He who had cast out many to lie unburied was himself unmourned; he had no funeral of any kind, no resting-place in the grave of his ancestors.

When news of this unrest reached the king, it became clear to him that Judea was in a state of rebellion. So he set out from Egypt in savage mood, took Yerushalayim by storm, and ordered his troops to cut down without mercy everyone they met and to slaughter those who took refuge in their houses. Young and old were murdered, women and children massacred, girls and infants butchered. At the end of three days their losses had amounted to eighty thousand, including forty thousand killed in battle and as many sold into slavery.

Not satisfied with this enormous carnage, the king had the audacity to enter the holiest temple on earth, guided by Menelaus, who had turned traitor both to his religion and his country. He laid impious hands on the sacred vessels; his desecrating hands swept together the votive offerings which other kings had set up to enhance the splendor and fame of the shrine.

The pride of Antiochus surpassed all bounds. He did not understand that the sins of the people of Yerushalayim had angered the Lord for a short time, and that this was why He left the *Mikdash* to its fate. If they had not already been guilty of many sinful acts, Antiochus would have had the same experience as Heliodorus who was sent by King Seleucus to inspect the treasury; like him he would have been scourged and his insolent plan foiled at once. But the Lord did not choose the nation for the sake of the sanctuary; he chose the sanctuary for the sake of the nation. Therefore even the sanctuary itself first had its part in the misfortunes that overtook the nation, and afterwards shared its good fortune. It was abandoned when the Lord Almighty was angry, but restored again in all its splendor when he became reconciled.

Antiochus, then, carried off eighteen hundred talents from the Temple and hastened back to Antioch. In his haughtiness he was rash enough to think that he could make ships sail on dry land and men walk over the sea. He left commissioners behind to oppress the Hebrews: in Yerushalayim Philip, by race a Phrygian, by disposition more barbarous than his master, and in Mount Gerizim Andronicus, to say nothing of Menelaus, who was even more brutal to the citizens than the others. Such was the king's hostility towards the Jews that he sent Apollonius, the general of the Mysian mercenaries, with an army of twenty-two thousand men, and ordered him to kill all the adult males and to sell the women and boys into slavery. When Apollonius arrived at Yerushalayim, he posed as a man of peace. He waited until the holy Shabbos day and, finding the Jews abstaining from work, he ordered a review of his troops. All who came out to see the parade he put to the sword; then, charging into the city with his soldiers, he killed a great number of people.

But Yehudah, also called Maccabbee, with about nine others, escaped into the desert, where he and his companions lived in the mountains, fending for themselves like the wild animals. They remained there living on what vegetation they found, so as to avoid the pollution in Yerushalayim.

Chapter Six
Shmad

Shortly afterwards King Antiochus sent an elderly Athenian to force the Jews to abandon their ancestral customs and cease regulating their lives according to the Torah. He was also commissioned to pollute the Temple at Yerushalayim and dedicate it to Olympian Zeus, and to dedicate the sanctuary on Mount Gerizim to Zeus God of Hospitality, following the practice of the local inhabitants.

This evil devastated the people; it was a severe trial. The

gentiles filled the *Beis HaMikdash* with licentious revelry: they took their pleasure with prostitutes and had intercourse with women in the sacred precincts. They also brought forbidden things inside, and heaped the altar with impure offerings prohibited by the law. It was forbidden either to observe the Shabbos or to keep the traditional festivals, or even to admit to being a Jew at all. On the monthly celebration of the king's birthday, the Jews were driven by brute force to eat the entrails of the sacrificial victims; on the feast of Dionysus they were forced to wear ivy-wreaths and join the procession in his honor. At the instigation of the inhabitants of Ptolemais an order was published in the neighboring Greek cities to the effect that they should adopt the same policy of compelling the Jews to eat sacrificial entrails, and should kill those who refused to change over to Greek ways.

Their miserable fate was there for all to see. For instance, two women were brought to trial for having had their children circumcised. They were paraded through the city, with their babies hanging at their breasts, and then flung down from the fortification. Other Jews had assembled in caves near Yerushalayim to keep the Shabbos in secret; they were denounced to Philip and were burnt alive, having refrained from defending themselves out of regard for the holiness of the day.

Now I beg my readers not to be disheartened by these calamities, but to reflect that such penalties were inflicted for the discipline of our race and not for its destruction. It is a sign of great kindness that acts of impiety should not be ignored for long but dealt with accordingly at once. The Lord did not see fit to deal with us as He does with the other nations: with them He patiently restrains His hand until they have reached the full extent of their sins, but upon us He inflicted retribution before our sins reached their height. So He never withdraws His mercy from us; though He disciplines His people by calamity, He never deserts them. It is enough for me to have interjected this truth; after this short digression, I must continue with my story.

There was Eleazar, one of the leading teachers of the law, a man of great age and distinguished bearing. He was being forced to open his mouth and eat pork, but preferring an honorable death to an unclean life; he spat it out and voluntarily submitted to the flogging, as indeed men should act who have the courage to refuse to eat forbidden food, even at the risk of their lives. For old acquaintance's sake, the officials in charge of this sacrilegious feast had a word with Eleazar in private; they urged him to bring meat which he was permitted to eat and had himself prepared, and only pretend to be eating the sacrificial meat as the king had ordered. In that way he would escape death and take advantage of the clemency which their long-standing friendship merited. But Eleazar made an honorable decision, one worthy of his years and the authority of old age, worthy of the gray hairs he had attained to and wore with such distinction, worthy of his perfect conduct from childhood up, but above all, worthy of the holy and God-given law. So he answered at once: 'Send me quickly to my grave. If I went through with this pretence at my time of life, many of the young might believe that at the age of ninety Eleazar had turned apostate. If I practiced deceit for the sake of a brief moment of life, I would lead them astray and dishonor my old age. I might for the present avoid man's punishment, but, alive or dead, I will never escape from the hand of the Almighty. So if I die bravely now, I will show that I have deserved my long life and will leave the young a fine example, to teach them how to die a good death, gladly and nobly, for our revered and holy laws.'

When he had finished speaking, he was immediately dragged away to be flogged. Those who a little while before had shown him friendship now became his enemies because, in their view, what he had said was madness. When he was almost dead from the blows, Eleazar sighed deeply and said: 'To the Lord belongs all holy knowledge. He knows what terrible agony I endure in my body from this flogging, though I could have escaped death; yet He knows also that in my soul I suffer gladly, because I stand in awe of Him.'

So he died; and by his death he left a heroic example and a glorious memory, not only for the young but also for the entire nation.

Chapter Seven
The Ultimate Sacrifice

Seven brothers with their mother had been arrested, and were being tortured by the king with whips and thongs to force them to eat pork, when one of them, speaking for all, said: 'What do you expect to learn by interrogating us? We are ready to die rather than break the laws of our fathers.' The king was enraged and ordered great pans and cauldrons to be heated up, and this was done at once. Then he gave orders that the tongue of the one that spoke first be cut out, and then his bodily extremities, before the eyes of his mother and his six brothers. This wreck of a man the king ordered to be taken, still breathing, to the fire and roasted in one of the pans. As the smoke from it streamed out far and wide, the mother and her sons encouraged each other to die nobly. 'The Lord God is watching', they said, 'and without doubt has compassion on us. Did not Moshe Rabbenu tell Yisrael to their faces in the song denouncing apostasy: "He will have compassion on his servants"?'

After the first brother had died in this way, the second was subjected to the same brutality. The skin and hair of his head were torn off, and he was asked: 'Will you eat, before we tear you limb from limb?' He replied in his native language, 'Never!', and so he in turn underwent the torture. With his last breath, he said: 'Fiend though you are, you are setting us free from this present life, and, since we die for His laws, the King of the universe will raise us up to a life forever renewed.'

After him the third was tortured. When the question was put to him, he at once spoke, boldly held out his hands, and said courageously: 'The God of heaven gave me these. His laws mean far more to me than my hands do, and it is from Him that I trust to receive them back.' When they heard this, the king and his followers were amazed at the young man's spirit and his utter disregard for suffering.

When he too was dead, they tortured the fourth in the same cruel way. At the point of death, he said to the king: 'Better to be killed by men and cherish God's promise to raise us again. There will be no resurrection to life for you!'

Then the fifth was dragged forward for torture. Looking at the king, he said: 'You have authority over men, mortal as you are, and can do as you please. But do not imagine that God has abandoned our race. Wait and see how His great power will torment you and your descendants.'

Next the sixth was brought, and said with his dying breath: 'Do not delude yourself. It is our own fault that we suffer these things; we have sinned against our God and brought these appalling disasters upon ourselves. But do not suppose you will escape the consequences of trying to fight against God.'

The mother was the most remarkable of all, and deserves to be remembered with special honor. She watched her seven sons all die in the space of a single day, yet she bore it bravely because she put her trust in the Lord. She encouraged each in turn in her native language. Filled with noble resolution, her woman's thoughts fired by a manly spirit, she said to them: 'You appeared in my womb, I know not how; it was not I who gave you life and breath and set in order your bodily frames. It is the Creator of the universe who molds man at his birth and plans the origin of all things. Therefore He, in His mercy, will give you back life and breath, since now you put His laws above all thought of self.'

Antiochus felt that he was being treated with contempt and suspected an insult in her words. The youngest brother was still left, and the king, not content with appealing to him, even assured him on oath that the moment he abandoned his ancestral customs he would make him rich and prosperous, by enrolling him as a King's Friend and entrusting him with high office. Since the young man paid no attention to him, the king summoned the mother and urged her to advise the lad to save his life. After much urging from the king, she agreed to persuade her son. She leaned towards him, and flouting the cruel tyrant, she said in their native language: 'My son, take pity on me. I carried you nine months in the womb, suckled you three years, reared you and brought you up to your present age. I beg you, child, look at the sky and the earth; see all that is in them and realize that God made them out of nothing, and that man comes into being in the same way. Do not be afraid of this butcher; accept death and prove yourself worthy of your brothers, so that by God's mercy I may receive you back along with them.'

She had barely finished when the young man spoke out:

'What are you all waiting for? I will not submit to the king's command; I obey the command of the law given by Moshe Rabbenu to our ancestors. And you, King Antiochus, who have devised all kinds of harm for the Hebrews, you will not escape God's hand. We are suffering for our own sins, and though to correct and discipline us our living Lord is angry for a short time, yet He will again be reconciled to His servants. But you, impious man, foulest of the human race, do not indulge vain hopes or be carried away by delusions of greatness, you who lay hands on God's servants. You are not yet safe from the judgment of the Almighty, all-seeing God. My brothers have now fallen in loyalty to God's covenant, after brief pain leading to eternal life; but you will pay the just penalty of your insolence by the verdict of God. I, like my brothers, surrender my body and my life for the laws of our fathers. I appeal to God to show mercy speedily to His people and by whips and scourges to bring you to admit that He alone is God. With me and my brothers may the Almighty's anger, which has justly fallen on all our race, be ended!'

The king, exasperated by these scornful words, was beside himself with rage. So he treated him worse than the others, and the young man died, putting his whole trust in the Lord, without having incurred defilement. Then finally, after her sons, the mother died.

This, then, must conclude our account of the eating of the entrails and the monstrous outrages that accompanied it.

---

entrails: obviously the text is confused here, since the story was about an attempt to make Jews eat pork

Chapter Eight
The Revolt

Meanwhile Yehudah, also called Maccabee, and his companions were making their way into the villages unobserved. They summoned their kinsmen and enlisted others who had remained faithful to Judaism, until they had collected about six thousand men. They invoked the Lord to look down and help His people, whom all were trampling under foot, to take pity on the *Beis HaMikdash* profaned by impious men, and to have mercy on Yerushalayim, which was being destroyed and would soon be leveled to the ground. They pleaded with Him also to listen to the blood that cried to Him for vengeance, to remember the infamous massacre of innocent children and the deeds of blasphemy against His name, and to show His hatred of wickedness.

Once his band of partisans was organized, Maccabee proved invincible to the gentiles, for the Lord's anger had changed to mercy. He came down on towns and villages without warning and burned them; he occupied the key positions and inflicted many severe reverses on the enemy, choosing the nighttime as being especially favorable for these attacks. His heroism was famous everywhere. When Philip realized that the small gains made by Yehudah were occurring with growing frequency, he wrote to Ptolemaeus, the governor of Coele-Syria and Phoenicia, asking for his help in protecting the royal interests. Ptolemaeus immediately selected Nicanor, son of Patroclus, a member of the highest order of King's Friends, and sent him at the head of at least twenty thousand troops of various nationalities to exterminate the entire Jewish race. Ptolemaeus appointed Gorgias, a highly experienced general, to join him. Nicanor determined to pay off the two thousand talents due from the king as tribute to the Romans, by the sale of the Jews he would take prisoner; and he at once made an offer of Jewish slaves to the coastal towns, undertaking to deliver them at the price of ninety to the talent. In his arrogance he never expected the vengeance of the Almighty, which he would soon experience.

World of Nicanor's advance reached Yehudah, and he informed his men that the enemy was approaching. The cowards who doubted God's justice fled. The rest disposed of their remaining possessions, and they prayed together to the Lord to save them from the impious Nicanor, who had sold them even before they met in battle. If they did not deserve to be saved based on their own merits, they invoked the covenants God had made with their ancestors who were faithful to His holy and majestic Name. Maccabee assembled his followers, six thousand in number, and appealed to them not to flee in panic before the enemy, nor to be afraid of the great host which was attacking them so unjustly. He encouraged them to fight nobly, always remembering the wicked crimes of the gentiles against the *Beis HaMikdash,* their callous outrage upon Yerushalayim, and, further, their suppression of their traditional Jewish way of life. 'They rely on their weapons and their audacity,' he said, 'but we rely on God Almighty, who can overthrow with a nod our present assailants and, if need be, the whole world.' He went on to recount to them the occasions when God had helped their ancestors, and how, in Sancheriv's time, one hundred and eighty-five thousand of the enemy had perished. He also spoke to them about the battle against the Galatians in Babylonia, when all the Jews engaged in the combat had numbered no more than eight thousand, with four thousand Macedonians, yet the Macedonians were thrown into confusion and the eight thousand through heaven's aid had destroyed one hundred and twenty thousand and taken much booty.

His words revived their courage, so that they were ready to die for their Torah and their country. He then divided the army into four units and gave each of his brothers, Shimon, Yosef, and Yonasan, command of a division of fifteen hundred men. In addition he appointed Eleazar to read the Torah aloud, and giving the signal for battle with the cry 'God is our help' and taking command of the leading division in person, he engaged Nicanor. The Almighty fought on their side, and they slaughtered over nine thousand of the enemy, wounded and disabled the greater part of Nicanor's forces, and defeated them completely. They seized the money of those who had come to buy them as slaves. After chasing the enemy a considerable distance, they were forced to stop because it was late; for it was Erev Shabbos, and for that reason they called off the pursuit. When they had collected the enemy's weapons and stripped the dead, they prepared to observe the Shabbos. They offered thanks and praises loud and long to the Lord who had been so merciful to them that day. After the Shabbos was over they distributed some of the spoils among the victims of persecution and the widows and orphans; the remainder they divided among themselves. This done, they all together pleaded to the merciful Lord, praying Him to be fully reconciled with His servants.

The Jews now engaged the forces of Timotheus and Bacchides and killed over twenty thousand. They gained complete control of some high strongholds, and divided the immense booty, giving shares equal to their own to the victims of persecution, to the widows and orphans, and to the old men as well. They carefully collected all the enemy's weapons, storing them at strategic points; the remainder of the spoils they brought into Yerushalayim. They killed the officer commanding the forces of Timotheus, an utterly godless man who had caused the Jews great suffering. During the victory celebrations in their capital, they burned alive the men who had set fire to the sacred gates, including Callisthenes, who had taken refuge in a small house; he thus received the appropriate punishment for his impiety.

Thus, with the Lord's help, Nicanor, that arch villain who had brought a thousand merchants to buy the Jewish captives, was humiliated by the very people whom he despised above all others. He threw off his magnificent uniform, and all alone, like a runaway slave, made his escape through the interior, and was, indeed, very lucky to reach Antioch after losing his whole army. So the man who had undertaken to pay the tribute to the Romans with slaves taken in Yerushalayim showed the world that the Jews had a Champion, and were therefore invulnerable because they kept the Torah He had given them.

Chapter Nine
The End of Antiochus

It so happened, about this time, that Antiochus returned in disorder from Persia. He had entered the city of Persepolis and attempted to plunder its temples and assume control. However, the populace rose and rushed to arms in their defence, with the result that Antiochus was routed by civilians and forced to beat a humiliating retreat. When he was near Ecbatana, news reached him of what had happened to Nicanor and the forces of Timotheus. Overcome with fury, he conceived the idea of making the Jews pay for the injury inflicted upon him by the Persians, who had made him flee; and so he ordered his charioteer to drive without stopping until the journey ended.

But he did not suspect that Divine judgment was riding with him! For in his arrogance he said: 'When I reach

Yerushalayim, I will make it a common graveyard for the Jews.' But the all-seeing Lord, the God of Yisrael, struck him a fatal and invisible blow. As soon as he had said the words, he was seized with incurable pain in his bowels, with sharp internal torments—a punishment entirely fitting for one who had inflicted many unheard-of torments on the bowels of others. Still he did not in the least control his insolence; more arrogant than ever, he furiously ranted and raved against the Jews. After he had given orders to speed up the journey, he fell out of his chariot as it hurtled along, and he fell so violently that every joint in his body was dislocated. He, who in his arrogance thought he could command the waves of the sea and weigh high mountains on the scales, was brought to the ground and had to be carried in a litter, thus making God's power manifest to all. Worms swarmed even from the eyes of this godless man and, while he was still alive and in agony, his flesh rotted off—the whole army was disgusted by the stench of his decay. It was so unbearably offensive that nobody could escort the man who, only a short time before, had seemed so powerful he could move the stars in the sky.

In this broken state, Antiochus began to rein in his great arrogance. Under God's lash and racked with continual pain, he began to see his situation clearly. He could not endure his own stench and said, 'It is right to submit oneself to God and, being mortal, not to think oneself equal to Him.' Then the villain made a solemn promise to the Lord—who had no intention of sparing him any longer—and it was to this effect: Yerushalayim the holy city, which he had been hurrying to level to the ground and to transform into a graveyard, he would now declare a free city. To all the Jews, whom he had not considered worthy of burial but only fit to be thrown out with their children as prey for birds and beasts, he would give privileges equal to those enjoyed by the citizens of Athens. The Holy Temple, which he had earlier plundered, he would adorn with the most splendid gifts; he would replace all the sacred utensils on a much more lavish scale; he would meet the cost of the sacrifices from his own revenues. In addition to all this, he would even become a Jew and visit every inhabited place to proclaim God's might.

When his pains in no way abated—because he was suffering from the judgment of God—he was in despair and, offering a desperate and final gesture, wrote to the Jews the letter copied here:

> 'To my worthy citizens, the Jews, warm greetings and good wishes for their health and prosperity from Antiochus, King and Chief Magistrate.
>
> 'May you and your children flourish and your affairs progress as you wish. Having my hope in heaven, I keep an affectionate remembrance of your regards and goodwill.
>
> 'As I was returning from Persia, I fell into a serious illness, and so I have judged it necessary to provide for the general safety of you all. Not that I despair of my condition—on the contrary, I have good hopes of recovery—but I observed that my father, whenever he made an expedition east of the Euphrates, appointed a successor, so that, if anything unexpected should happen or if some troublesome report should spread, his subjects would not be disturbed, since they would know to whom the empire had been left. Further, I know well that the neighboring princes on the frontiers of my kingdom are watching for an opportunity and waiting on events. So I have designated as king my son Antiochus, whom I frequently entrusted and recommended to most of you during my regular visits to the satrapies beyond the Euphrates. I have written to him what is here copied. Wherefore I pray and entreat each one of you to maintain your existing goodwill

towards myself and my son, remembering the services I have rendered to you both as a community and as individuals. For I am sure my son will follow my own policy of moderation and benevolence and will accommodate himself to your wishes.'

Thus this murderer and blasphemer, suffering the worst of agonies, such as he had made others suffer, met a pitiable end in the mountains of a foreign land. His body was brought back by Philip, his intimate friend; but he was afraid of Antiochus's son and went over to Ptolemy Philometor in Egypt.

Chapter Ten
Rebuilding

Maccabee with his men, led by the Lord, recovered the *Beis HaMikdash* and the city of Yerushalayim. He demolished the altars erected by the heathen in the public square, and their sacred precincts as well. When they had purified the sanctuary, they constructed a new altar; then, striking fire from flints, they offered a *korban* for the first time in two whole years, and restored the *ketores,* the Menorah, and the *Lechem HaPanim*. This done, they prostrated themselves and prayed to the Lord not to let them experience any further disasters, but, should they ever happen to sin, to discipline them Himself with clemency and not hand them over to blasphemous and barbarous gentiles. The sanctuary was purified on the twenty-fifth of Kislev, the same day of the same month as that on which foreigners had profaned it. The joyful celebration lasted for eight days; it was like the *Yom Tov* of Sukkos, for they recalled how, only a short time before, they had kept that feast while they were living like wild animals in the mountains and caves. Therefore they carried garlands of flowers and branches with their fruits, as well as palm-fronds, and they chanted hymns to the One who had so triumphantly achieved the purification of His own *Mikdash*. A measure was passed by the Sanhedrin to the effect that the entire Jewish people should keep these days every year.

We have already recounted the end of Antiochus, who was called Epiphanes. Now we will describe what happened under that godless man's son, Antiochus Eupator, in a brief summary of the principal evils brought about by his wars. At his accession, Eupator appointed as his vizier a man called Lysias, who had succeeded Ptolemaeus Macron as governor-general of Coele-Syria and Phoenicia. For Ptolemaeus had taken the lead in reversing the former unjust treatment of the Jews and had attempted to maintain peaceful relations with them, and as a result he was denounced by the King's Friends to Eupator. On every side he was called traitor, because he had abandoned Cyprus, entrusted to him by Philometor, and had gone over to Antiochus Epiphanes. He still enjoyed power but no longer had respect, and in despair he ended his life by poison.

When Gorgias became governor, he engaged mercenaries and took every opportunity to attack the Jews. At the same time, the Idumaeans, who were in control of strategic fortresses, were also harassing them; they harbored renegades from Yerushalayim and carried on the war. Maccabee and his men conducted a public supplication and prayed to God to fight on their side. They made a vigorous assault on the Idumaean fortresses and captured them; they drove off all who were manning the walls, and killed at least twenty thousand of the enemy.

Epiphanes: Greek, "the divine manifestation"

Nine thousand or more of the enemy took refuge in two towers, very strongly fortified and fully equipped against a siege. Maccabee himself set out for the places where his troops needed him, but left Shimon and Yosef behind with Zakkai and his men. These leaders were sufficient to conduct the siege, but Shimon's men were too fond of money, and when they were bribed with seventy thousand drachmas by some men in the towers, they let them slip through their lines. When Maccabee was informed of this, he assembled the leaders of the army and denounced these men for having sold their brothers for money by letting their enemies escape. Then he executed the traitors, and immediately captured the two towers. His military operations were completely successful; between the two fortresses he destroyed over twenty thousand of the enemy.

After his previous defeat by the Jews, Timotheus collected a huge force of mercenaries and Asian cavalry, advancing to take Judea by storm. As he approached, Maccabee and his men prayed to God. They sprinkled dust on their heads and put sackcloth around their waists; they prostrated themselves at the base of the altar and begged God to favor them, 'to be an enemy of their enemies and an opponent of their opponents', as the law clearly states.

When they had finished their prayer, they took up their weapons, advanced a good distance from Yerushalayim, and halted near the enemy. At first light the two armies engaged in battle. For the Jews, success and victory were guaranteed not only because of their bravery, but even more because the Lord was their refuge, whereas the gentiles had only their own fury to lead them into battle. As the fighting grew more intense, the enemy saw in the sky five magnificent

---

twenty thousand: the figures in these pages are somewhat confused

figures riding horses with golden bridles, who placed themselves at the head of the Jews, formed a circle round Maccabee, and kept him invulnerable under the protection of their armor. They launched arrows and thunderbolts at the enemy, who, confused and blinded, broke their ranks in complete disorder. Twenty thousand and five hundred of the infantry, as well as six hundred cavalry, were slaughtered.

Timotheus himself fled to a fortress called Gezer, commanded by Chaereas and strongly garrisoned. Maccabee and his men welcomed this advantage, and for four days they laid siege to the place. The garrison, confident in the strength of their position, hurled horrible and impious blasphemies at them, until, at dawn on the fifth day, twenty young men from Maccabee's force, burning with rage at the blasphemy, courageously stormed the wall and, in savage anger, cut down all that they met. Under cover of this distraction others got up the same way, attacked the defenders, set fire to the towers, and in the fires they had started they burned the blasphemers alive. Others broke down the gates and let in the rest of the army, and thus the city was occupied. Timotheus had hidden himself in a cistern, but he was killed along with his brother Chaereas and Apollophanes. To celebrate their achievement, the Jews praised with hymns and thanksgivings the Lord who showers blessings on Yisrael and gives them the victory.

---

this advantage: of having the enemy commander cooped up in one place

Chapter Eleven
Lysias Defeated

The vice regent Lysias, the king's guardian and relative, was angered by these events. Very shortly afterwards he collected about eighty thousand troops, in addition to his entire cavalry, and advanced on the Jews. He planned on making Yerushalayim a settlement for gentiles, subjecting the Temple to taxation like all gentile shrines, and putting up the high-priesthood for sale annually. He reckoned not at all with the might of God, but was awed by his own myriads of infantry, his thousands of cavalry, and his eighty elephants. Penetrating into Judea, he approached Beit Tzur, a fortified place about twenty miles from Yerushalayim, and closely besieged it.

When Maccabee and his men learned that Lysias was besieging their fortresses, they and all the people, wailing and weeping, prayed to the Lord to send a good angel to deliver Yisrael. Maccabee was the first to arm himself, and he urged the rest to join the battle and come to the aid of their brothers. One and all they set out eagerly. They were still in the neighborhood of Yerushalayim when there appeared at their head a horseman arrayed in white, brandishing his golden weapons. Then with one voice they praised their merciful God, and felt so spiritually strong that they could have breached walls of iron and attacked not only men, but also the most savage animals. They came on fully armed, with their heavenly ally, under the mercy of the Lord. They hurled themselves like lions against the enemy, killing eleven thousand, as well as sixteen hundred cavalry, and putting all the rest to flight. Most of those who escaped lost their weapons and were wounded, and Lysias saved his life only by running away.

However, Lysias was no fool, and when he analyzed the defeat he had suffered he realized that the Hebrews were invincible, because God fought on their side. He proposed a settlement consisting of entirely acceptable terms, promising also to win the king over by putting pressure on him to show friendship to the Jews. Maccabee agreed to all the proposals of Lysias out of regard for the general welfare, for the king had accepted all the proposals from the Jewish side which Maccabee had forwarded to Lysias in writing.

The letter of Lysias to the Jews ran as follows:

'Lysias to the Jewish community, greeting.

'Your representatives Yochanan and Avshalom have handed to me the document here copied and have asked me to ratify what is contained in it. Whatever needed to be brought to the king's knowledge I have communicated to him, and what was within my own competence I have granted. If, therefore, you maintain your goodwill towards the empire, I for my part will endeavor to promote your welfare for the future. I have ordered your representatives and mine to confer with you about the details. Farewell.

The twenty-fourth of Dioscorus in the year 148.'

The king's letter ran as follows:

'King Antiochus to his brother Lysias, greeting.

'Now that our royal father has gone to join the gods, we desire that our subjects be undisturbed in the conduct of their own affairs. We have learned that the

---

the year 148: 164 BCE

Jews do not consent to adopt Greek ways, as our father wished, but prefer their own mode of life and request that they be allowed to observe their own laws. We choose, therefore, that this nation, like the rest, should be left undisturbed, and decree that their Temple be restored to them and that they shall regulate their lives in accordance with their ancestral customs. Have the goodness, therefore, to inform them of this and ratify it, so that, knowing what our intentions are, they may settle down confidently and quietly to manage their own affairs.'

To the people the king's letter ran thus:

'King Antiochus to the Jewish Senate and people, greeting.

'We hope that you prosper. We too are in good health. Menelaus has informed us of your desire to return to your own homes. Therefore we declare an amnesty for all who return before the thirtieth of Xanthicus. The Jews may follow their own food-laws as heretofore, and none of them shall be charged with any previous infringement. I am sending Menelaus to reassure you. Farewell.

The fifteenth of Xanthicus in the year 148.'

The Romans also sent the Jews the following letter:

'Quintus Memmius and Titus Manius, Roman legates, to the Jewish people, greeting.

'We give our assent to all that Lysias, the king's relative, has granted you. But examine carefully the ques-

---

the year 148: 164 BCE

tions which he reserved for reference to the king; then send someone immediately, so that we may make suitable proposals, for we are proceeding to Antioch. Send messengers therefore without delay, so that we also may know your opinion. Farewell.

The fifteenth of Xanthicus in the year 148.'

Chapter Twelve
Gorgias' Attempt

When these agreements had been concluded, Lysias went off to the king, and the Jews returned to their farming. But some of the governors in the region, namely Timotheus and Apollonius son of Gennaeus, and also Hieronymus and Demophon, and in addition Nicanor, chief of the Cypriot mercenaries, would not allow them to enjoy security and live in peace.

I must now describe an atrocity committed by the inhabitants of Yafo. They invited the Jews living in the town to embark, with their wives and children, in boats which they provided, with no indication of any ill will towards them. As it was a public decision by the whole town, and because they wished to live in peace and suspected nothing, they accepted; but when they were out at sea the people of Yafo sank the boats, drowning no fewer than two hundred of them. When Yehudah learned of this brutal treatment of his fellow-countrymen, he alerted his troops, invoked God, the just judge, and fell upon their murderers. He set the harbor of Yafo on fire at night, burned the ships, and killed those who had taken refuge there. But finding the town gates closed, he withdrew—intending, however, to return and root out the entire community. When he learned that the people of Yavneh intended to do the same to the Jews who lived among them, he attacked Yavneh by night and set fire to its harbor and fleet; the light of the flames was visible in Yerushalayim, thirty miles away.

When they had marched more than a mile further in their advance against Timotheus, they were set upon by not less than five thousand Arabs, with five hundred cavalry. A violent combat ensued, in which, by Divine help, Yehudah and his men were victorious. The defeated nomads begged Yehudah to make an alliance with them, and promised to supply him with cattle and to give the Jews every other assistance. Yehudah realized that they could indeed be useful in many ways; so he agreed to make peace with them, and, after receiving assurances from him, they returned to their tents.

Yehudah also attacked Caspin, a walled town, strongly fortified and inhabited by a motley crew of gentiles. Confident in the strength of their walls and in their store of provisions, the defenders provoked Yehudah and his men, abusing them and also uttering the most wicked blasphemies. But the Jews invoked the world's great Sovereign, who in the days of Yehoshua threw down the walls of Yericho without battering rams or siege engines. They attacked the wall fiercely and by the will of God captured the town. The carnage was indescribable: the adjacent lake, a quarter of a mile wide, appeared to be flowing with blood.

Advancing about ninety-five miles from there, they reached Charax, which is inhabited by the Tubian Jews, as they are called. They did not find Timotheus there; he had left the district by that time, having had no success, but in one place he had left behind an extremely strong garrision. Dositheus and Sosipater, Maccabee's generals, set out and destroyed the garrison, which consisted of over ten thousand men. Maccabee, for his part, grouped his army in several divisions, appointed commanders for them, and hurried after Timotheus, whose forces numbered a hundred and twenty thousand infantry and two thousand five hundred cavalry. When he learned of Yehudah's approach, Timotheus sent off the women and children with all the baggage to a town called Karnayim, this being an inaccessible place, hard to storm because all the approaches to it were narrow. But when Yehudah's first division appeared, terror and panic seized the enemy, as the All-seeing One decreed. In their flight the enemy rushed headlong in every direction, so that frequently they were injured by their comrades or were run through by each other's swords. Yehudah conducted the pursuit vigorously and killed thirty thousand of these criminals. Timotheus himself was taken prisoner by the troops of Dositheus and Sosipater. With much cunning he begged them to let him go in safety, pointing out that most of them had parents, and some of them brothers, who were in his hands, and who might never be heard of again. He pledged himself over and over again to restore these hostages safe and sound; and so they let him go in order to save their relatives.

Yehudah moved on to Karnayim itself and the sanctuary of Atargatis, and killed twenty-five thousand people there. After this victory and destruction he next marched on Ephron, a fortified town inhabited by a mixed population. Stalwart young men took up their position in front of the walls and fought vigorously, confident in their great supply of war engines and ammunition. But the Jews invoked the Sovereign whose might shatters all the strength of the enemy, and killed twenty-five thousand of the defenders, asserting their authority over the town. Then they advanced to Scythopolis, some seventy-five miles from Yerushalayim. The Jews who lived there testified to the goodwill shown them by the people of Scythopolis and the kindness with which they had treated them during difficult times; so Yehudah and his men thanked them, charged them to be equally friendly to the Jewish race in the future, and then returned to Yerushalayim in time for Shavuos.

After celebrating Shavuos, as it is called, they advanced to attack Gorgias, the general in charge of Idumea, who met them with three thousand infantry and four hundred cavalry. When the ranks joined battle, a small number of the Jews fell. But Dositheus, a Tubian Jew and cavalryman of great strength, grabbed Gorgias by his cloak and was dragging the villain off, intending to take him alive, when a Thracian horseman bore down on him and chopped off his arm; so Gorgias escaped to Marisa.

Gorgias' men had been fighting continuously and were exhausted, when Yehudah invoked the Lord to show Himself their ally and leader in battle. Singing hymns in his native language as a battle-cry, he put the forces of Gorgias to flight by a surprise attack.

Regrouping his forces, he led them to the town of Adullam. The seventh day was approaching, so they purified themselves, as custom dictated, and kept the Shabbos there. Next day they went, as had by now become necessary, to collect the bodies of the fallen in order to bury them with their relatives in the ancestral graves. But on every one of the dead, they found, under each tunic, amulets sacred to the idols of Yavneh, objects which the Torah forbids to Jews. It was evident to all that here was the reason why these men had fallen. Therefore they praised the work of the Lord, the just judge, who reveals what is hidden; and, turning to prayer, they asked that this sin might be entirely blotted out and forgotten. The noble Yehudah called on the people to refrain from sin, for they had seen with their own eyes what had happened to the fallen because of their sin. He levied a contribution from each man, and sent the total of two thousand silver shekels to Yerushalayim for a sin-offering—an appropriate action in which he took due account of the resurrection. For if he had not hoped that the fallen would some day rise again, it would have been foolish and superfluous to pray for the dead. But since he had in view the wonderful reward reserved for those who die an honorable death, his purpose was a holy and pious one. And this was why Yehudah offered an atoning sacrifice to cleanse the dead from their sin.

Chapter Thirteen
The Treason of Menelaus

In the year 149 information reached Yehudah and his men that Antiochus Eupator was advancing on Judea with a large army; he was accompanied by Lysias, his guardian and vizier, along with a Greek force consisting of one hundred and ten thousand infantry, five thousand three hundred cavalry, twenty-two elephants, and three hundred chariots equipped with scythes.

Menelaus also joined them and urged Antiochus on; this he did for dishonest reasons: not for his country's good, but because he believed he would thereby be sure to maintain his position in office. However, the King of kings aroused the rage of Antiochus against Menelaus: Lysias produced evidence that the criminal was responsible for all Antiochus's troubles, and so the king ordered that he be taken to Beroea

---

the year 149: 163 BCE

"scythes": sword blades attached to the spokes of the wheels, so as to rotate and cut anyone within their reach to pieces

and there be executed in the manner customary at that place. This is, that in Beroea there is a tower some seventy-five feet high, filled with ashes; it has a circular structure sloping down on all sides into the ashes. This is where the citizens take someone guilty of sacrilege or any other notorious crime, and throw him to his death. Such was the fate of the law-breaker Menelaus, who was not even allowed burial —a fate he richly deserved. Many times he had desecrated the hallowed ashes of the altar-fire, and by ashes he met his death.

So the king advanced with the barbarous intention of inflicting on the Jews sufferings far worse than his father had inflicted. When Yehduah heard this he ordered the people to invoke the Lord day and night and pray that now, more than ever, He would come to their aid and prevent them from falling into the hands of the blaspheming gentiles. They were in danger of losing the Torah, their country, and the *Beis HaMikdash*, so He should not desert them just when they had begun to breath again. They all obeyed Yehudah's orders: for three days without respite they prayed to their merciful Lord, they wailed, fasted and prostrated themselves. Then Yehudah urged them to action and called upon them to stand by him.

After holding a council of war with the elders, he decided not to wait until the royal army invaded Judea and took Yerushalayim, but to march out and with God's help to take the offensive. He entrusted the outcome to the Creator of the world; his troops he charged to fight bravely to the death for the Torah, for the *Mikdash* and for Yerushalayim, for their country and their way of life. He pitched camp near Modi'in, and giving his men the signal for battle with the cry 'God's victory!', he made a night attack on the royal pavilion with a select force of the bravest young men. He killed as many as two thousand in the enemy camp, and his men stabbed to death the leading elephant and its driver. In the end they reduced the whole camp to panic and confusion, and withdrew victorious. It was all over by daybreak, through the help and protection which Yehudah had received from the Lord.

Now that he had had a taste of Jewish daring, the king tried stratagems in attacking their strong-points. He advanced on Beit Tzur, one of their powerful forts, and attacked, but was beaten. Yehudah sent in supplies to the garrison, but Rhodocus, a soldier in the Jewish ranks, betrayed their secrets to the enemy. However, he was tracked down, arrested, and put away. The king parleyed for the second time with the inhabitants of Beit Tzur, and when he had given and received guarantees, he withdrew; he then attacked Yehudah and his men, but had the worst of it. He now received news that Philip, whom he had left in charge of state affairs in Antioch, had gone out of his mind. In dismay he summoned the Jews, agreed to their terms, took an oath to respect all their rights, and after this settlement offered a sacrifice, paid honor to the sanctuary and its precincts, and received Maccabee graciously. He left Hegemonides behind as governor of the region from Ptolemais to Gerra, and went himself to Ptolemais. Its inhabitants were furious at the treaty he had made, and in their alarm wanted to repudiate it. Lysias mounted the rostrum, made the best defense he could, won the people over, calmed them down, and, having thus gained their support, left for Antioch.

Such was the course of the king's offensive and retreat.

Chapter Fourteen
Victory over Nicanor

After an interval of three years, information reached Yehudah and his men that Demetrius son of Seleucus had sailed into the harbor of Tripolis with a powerful army and fleet, and, after disposing of Antiochus and his guardian Lysias, had taken possession of the country.

There was a man called Alcimus, who had formerly been High Priest but had submitted voluntarily to pollutions at the time of the secession. This man, realizing that now there was not the slightest guarantee of his safety, or any possibility of regaining access to the holy altar, came to King Demetrius, about the year 151, and presented him with a gold crown and palm, and also some of the customary olive branches from the *Beis HaMikdash*. On that particular occasion he kept quiet; but he found a chance of forwarding his own mad scheme when Demetrius summoned him to his council and questioned him about the attitude and plans of the Jews. He replied: 'Those of the Jews who are called Chassidim and are led by Yehudah Maccabee are keeping the war alive and fomenting sedition, refusing to leave the kingdom in peace. Thus, although I have been deprived of my hereditary official capacity—I mean the high-priesthood—I am here today with two motives: first, a genuine concern for the king's rights; and secondly, a regard for my fellow-citizens, since our whole race is suffering considerable hardship as a result of the folly of the people I have just mentioned. I would advise your majesty to acquaint yourself with every one of these matters and then make provision for our country and our beleaguered nation, as befits your universal

---

the year 151: 161 BCE

kindness and goodwill. For the empire will enjoy no peace so long as Yehudah remains alive.'

When he had spoken to this effect, the other Friends, who were hostile to Yehudah, immediately inflamed Demetrius still more. The king at once selected Nicanor, commander of the elephant corps, gave him command of Judea, and sent him off with a commission to dispose of Yehudah and disperse his forces, and to install Alcimus as High Priest of the great Temple. The gentile population of Judea, refugees from the attacks of Yehudah, now flocked to Nicanor, thinking that defeat and misfortune for the Jews would mean prosperity for themselves.

When the Jews learned of Nicanor's offensive and that the gentiles had joined his forces, they sprinkled dust over themselves and prayed to the One who established His people for ever, who never fails to manifest Himself when His chosen are in need of help. At their leader's command, they immediately struck camp and joined battle with the enemy at the village of Hadassah. Shimon, Yehudah's brother, had fought an engagement with Nicanor, but because the enemy came up unexpectedly he had suffered a slight reverse. In spite of this, when Nicanor learned how brave Yehudah and his troops were and how courageously they fought for their country, he shrank from deciding the issue in battle. So he sent Posidonius, Theodotus, and Mattathias to negotiate a settlement.

After a lengthy consideration of the proposals, Yehudah informed his men of the settlement, and they were unanimous in agreeing to make peace. A day was fixed for a private meeting of the leaders. A chariot advanced from each of the two lines, and seats were placed for them, but Yehudah posted armed men at strategic points ready to deal with any unforeseen treachery on the enemy's part. The discussion between the two leaders was harmonious. Nicanor stayed some time in Yerushalayim and behaved correctly; he dismissed the crowds that flocked round him, and kept Yehudah always close to himself. He had acquired a real affection for him, and urged him to marry and start a family. So Yehudah married and settled down to the quiet life of an ordinary citizen.

Alcimus noticed their friendliness and got hold of a copy of the agreement they had concluded. He went to Demetrius and said that Nicanor was pursuing a policy detrimental to the interests of the empire, by appointing that traitor Yehudah a King's Friend. The king was furious; he was provoked by these villainous slanders to write to Nicanor, expressing his dissatisfaction with the agreement and ordering him to arrest Maccabee and send him at once to Antioch. This message filled Nicanor with dismay; he was very reluctant to break his agreement, since the man had committed no offence, but since there was no going against the king, he watched for a favorable opportunity to carry out the order by means of some stratagem. Maccabee, however, observed that Nicanor had become less friendly towards him and no longer showed him the same civility. He realized that this unfriendliness boded no good, so he collected a large number of his followers and went into hiding from Nicanor.

When Nicanor recognized that he had been outmaneuvered by the resolute action of Yehudah, he went to the great and holy *Mikdash* at the time when the *Cohanim* were offering the day's *korbanos* and ordered them to surrender Yehudah to him. The priests declared on oath that they did not know the whereabouts of the wanted man. But Nicanor stretched out his right hand towards the *Kodesh* and swore this oath: 'Unless you surrender Yehudah into my custody, I will raze God's sanctuary to the ground, I will destroy the altar, and on this spot I will build a temple to Dionysus for all the world to see.' With these words he left; but the priests, with outstretched hands, prayed to Heaven, the constant Champion of our people: 'Lord, You have no need of anything in the world, yet it was Your will that among us there should be a shrine to be Your dwelling-place. Now, Lord who alone are holy, keep this house, so newly purified, forever free from defilement.'

Razis, a *dayan* of the Sanhedrin, was denounced to Nicanor. He was very highly regarded, a patriot and a man whose generosity had earned him the name 'Father of the Jews.' In the early days of the secession he had stood his trial for practicing Judaism, and with the utmost eagerness had risked life and limb for that cause. Nicanor wished to give clear proof of his hostility towards the Jews, and sent more than five hundred soldiers to arrest Razis; he reckoned that his arrest would be a severe blow to the people. The troops were on the point of capturing the tower where Razis was, and were trying to force the outer door. Then an order was given to set the door on fire, and Razis, hemmed in on all sides, turned his sword on himself. He preferred to die nobly rather than fall into the hands of criminals and be subjected to gross humiliation. In his haste and anxiety he misjudged the blow, and with the troops pouring through the doors he ran without hesitation on to the wall and heroically threw himself down into the crowd. The crowd hurriedly gave way and he fell in the space they left. He was still breathing, still on fire with courage; so, streaming with blood and severely wounded, he picked himself up and dashed through the crowd. Finally, standing on a sheer rock, and now completely drained of blood, he took his entrails in both hands and flung them at the crowd. And thus, invoking the Lord of life and breath to give these entrails back to him again, he died.

Nicanor received information that Yehudah and his men

were in the region of Samaria, and he determined to attack them on their day of rest, when it could be done without any danger. Those Jews who were forced to accompany his army said, 'Do not carry out such a savage and barbarous massacre, but respect the day singled out and made holy by the All-seeing One.' The arch villain retorted, 'Is there indeed a ruler in the sky who has ordered the Sabbath day to be observed?' The Jews declared, 'The living Lord Himself is ruler in the sky, and He ordered the seventh day to be kept holy.' 'But I', replied Nicanor, 'am a ruler on earth, and I order you to take your arms and do your duty to the king.' However, he did not succeed in carrying out his cruel plan.

Now Nicanor, in his pretentious and extravagant conceit, had resolved to erect a public trophy from the spoils of Yehudah's forces. But Maccabee's confidence never wavered, and he had not the least doubt that he would obtain help from the Lord. He urged his men not to be afraid of the gentile attack, but to bear in mind the aid they had received from Heaven in the past, and so to look to the Almighty for the victory which He would send this time also. He encouraged them by quoting from the law and the prophets; and, by reminding them of the battles they had already won, filled them with a fresh enthusiasm. When he had renewed their courage, he gave them their orders, reminding them at the same time of the gentiles' broken faith and perjury. He armed each one of them, not so much with the security of shield and spear, as with the encouragement that brave words bring; and he also told them of a trustworthy dream he had had, a sort of waking vision, which further inspired them.

What he had seen was this: the former High Priest Onias

---

when it could be done...: or so he imagined

appeared to him, that good man of modest bearing and mild disposition, the apt speaker and exponent of right action from childhood. With outstretched hands he was praying earnestly for the whole community. Then Yehudah saw another man praying, a figure of great age and dignity, whose wonderful air of authority marked him as a man of the utmost distinction. Then Onias said, 'This is God's prophet Yirmiyah, who loves his fellow Jews and offers many prayers for our people and for the Holy City.' Yirmiyah extended his right hand and delivered to Yehudah a golden sword, saying as he did so, 'Take this holy sword, the gift of God, and with it crush your enemies.'

The eloquent words of Yehudah had the power of stimulating everyone to bravery and making men out of boys. Encouraged by them, the Jews made up their minds not to remain in camp, but to take the offensive manfully and fight hand to hand with all their strength until the issue was decided. This they did because Yerushalayim, their religion, and their *Mikdash* were in danger. Their fear was not chiefly for their wives and children, still less for brothers and relatives, but first and foremost for the *Beis HaMikdash*. The distress of those shut up in Yerushalayim was no less, for they were anxious at the prospect of a battle on open ground.

All were waiting for the decisive struggle ahead. The enemy had already concentrated his forces; his army was drawn up in order of battle, the elephants stationed in a favorable position and the cavalry ranged on the flank. When Maccabee observed the deployment of the troops, the variety of their equipment, and the ferocity of the elephants, with hands upraised he invoked the Lord, the worker of miracles; for he knew that God grants victory to those who deserve it, not because of their military strength, but as He Himself decides. This was his prayer: *'Ribbono shel Olam,*

You sent Your angel in the days of King Chizkiah of Yehudah, and he killed as many as a hundred and eighty-five thousand men in Sancheriv's camp. Now, Ruler of Heaven, send a good angel once again to go before us, spreading fear and panic. May they be struck down by Your strong arm, these blasphemers who are coming to attack Your holy people!' Thus he ended.

Nicanor and his forces advanced with trumpets and war-cries, but Yehudah and his men joined battle with invocations and prayers. Fighting hand-to-hand and praying to God in their hearts, they killed no fewer than thirty-five thousand men, and were greatly cheered by the divine intervention.

The action was over, and they were joyfully disbanding, when they recognized Nicanor lying dead in his armor. Then with tumultuous shouts they praised their Master in their native language. Yehudah their leader, who had always fought body and soul on behalf of his fellow-Jews, never losing his youthful patriotism, now ordered Nicanor's head to be cut off, also his hand and arm, and taken to Yerushalayim. When he arrived he summoned all the people and stationed the priests before the altar. Then he sent for the men in the citadel, and showed them the head of the infamous and vicious Nicanor, and the hand which this bragging blasphemer had extended against the Almighty's *Mikdash*. He cut out the tongue of the impious Nicanor, and said he would give it to the birds bit by bit; and he gave orders that the evidence of what Nicanor's folly had brought upon him should be hung up opposite the *Beis HaMikdash*. They all made the sky ring with the praises of the Lord who had shown His power: 'Praise to Him who has preserved His own sanctuary from defilement!' Yehudah hung Nicanor's head from the citadel, a clear proof of the Lord's help, for all to see. It was unanimously decreed that this day should never pass unnoticed, but be regularly celebrated. It is the thirteenth of the twelfth month, called Adar in Aramaic, the day before Mordechai's Day. Such, then, was the fate of Nicanor, and from that time Yerushalayim has remained in the possession of the Hebrews.

At this point I will bring my work to an end. If it is considered well-written and aptly composed, that is what I myself hoped for; if superficial and mediocre, I could only do my best. For just as it is disagreeable to drink wine alone or water alone, whereas the mixing of the two gives a pleasant and delightful taste, so too, variety of style in a literary work charms the ear of the reader. Let this then be my final word.

A Second Look

Books, Authors, and History

Notes On How We Know What Really Happened

by
Rabbi Yaakov Lavon

Most people think of history as the record of what happened in previous generations. I would prefer to call it the art of attempting to find out what *really* happened. The task is no easy one: ask any policeman if he has ever heard two people give the same account of an accident they witnessed. He'll tell you it has never happened. Then ask a judge how often witnesses lie, even under oath; "Quite often," he'll tell you. Now ask him how often witnesses give a twisted version of their testimony — a version that reflects more their prejudices than the facts. "Practically always" will be the answer.

What does this say about history? After all, history consists entirely of what people tell us they saw and heard. How much of it is true, then, and *how* true is it?[1] Getting some kind of answer to these questions is the historian's art. And, as with any art, the result will be very much a matter of taste.

Sometimes things go easily: there are periods from which several accounts survive, and then we can compare them and see which bits everyone agrees about and which are disputed. Or we may have an account from someone his contemporaries considered an honorable man. Not that either of these cases gives us any guarantee of truth. A whole society may lie about some things (such as racism and social inequalities); and a seemingly honorable man may be found in the

---

1 This question is no new one. The great 14th-century Persian historian ibn Batuta wrote a three-volume *Al-muqqadima* ("Preface") to his world history, just to offer an answer. Needless to say, his "definitive resolution" to the problem is largely discredited nowadays.

end to be a rogue. But at least in cases like these we can make a start.

Then there are other periods, from which little has survived. The Second Temple period is one of these. During the bloody infighting among the descendants of Herod, much of the country was laid waste and priceless records and documents perished, along with still more precious human lives — and memories. Then, after the disastrous wars with the Romans, little was left of Eretz Yisrael except ashes and rubble. The Romans were furious with the little country that would not submit like the rest of the world, and the extent of the destruction they did in revenge is almost impossible to conceive. It was nearly total: the country was literally burnt to ashes. Whatever records had existed were gone forever, and those who could have dictated live memoirs were dead, either under the ruins of sacked cities or in the Roman circuses.

How, then, do we know anything about this period? We have the occasional mention by a Greek or Roman author, who wrote almost always with disdain and never with any understanding. We have, of course, whatever Chazal decided to recount; but that is not much, because Chazal's purpose is to teach Torah, not history.

And then we have a few of the most confounded books ever seen: books which pretend to give a complete account of these times, but which are open to any and every criticism, suspicion, and doubt.

We can consider first the writings of Flavius Josephus, originally known as Yoseph ben Mattisyahu ben Gurion, alias Yosipon. Setting aside my personal loathing for this despicable traitor, there are several objective problems that anyone needs to consider before drawing on Josephus' histories.

The first is his unsatisfactory personality, at once unstable and unsavory. This must cast doubt on both his probity and his reliability — that is, even if he is not lying or irresponsibly exaggerating (and he does both frequently), we do not know how much he ever troubled himself to give an accurate account. R. Chaim Ozer Grodszensky זצ"ל considered this the primary problem with Josephus.²

Then there is the text itself. Immediately our problem gets more complicated, because most Jews know of Josephus only from a book called *Sefer Yosipon* — which Flavius Josephus definitely did not write. (It is rare for a historian to be able to state anything definitely, so I will make the most of this occasion.) The evidence is simple enough: the sentence structure and the grammatical forms in this book all belong to the Middle Ages, long after Josephus was dead. Now, however individual writing styles may be, it is impossible for a man to use words and forms that won't be invented until centuries later, and since *Sefer Yosipon* is full of such forms Josephus could not have written it. Some later man concocted it as an edited abridgement of several of Josephus' actual works; it certainly does not represent what the man himself wrote.

What, then, of Josephus' actual writings? One difficulty is that they are all in Greek; another is that the extant manuscripts are not always very good; and a third is that there are many variant readings. In *The Jewish War* there are several whole passages (concerning the origins of Christianity) which appear only in the Slavonic group of manuscripts. All in all, there are enough problems with the Josephus texts that we are often in doubt what he actually said.

Again, even if we know the correct text, we must remember that this text itself is a translation. Josephus needed to write in Greek, because that was the learned language of the day, and so his books would be read with respect.³ But whether or not he wrote his Greek books himself, he was

---

2 Heard from my Rosh Yeshivah, R. Yisrael Z'ev Gustman הכ"מ.

3 Much as, in later days in Europe, Latin was the learned language and serious scholarly books had to be written in Latin.

unquestionably thinking in Aramaic the whole time. Now, when a man knows a foreign language really well, he thinks in that language while he speaks it, with the result that he speaks both gracefully and accurately. If he does not know the language well, he continues to think in his native language, translating mentally phrase by phrase as he goes, with the result that he speaks awkwardly and imprecisely. He is liable to say something that is not quite what he meant, without ever knowing it. It is evident that Josephus does this all the time.

Why does he do it? There are two possibilities. One is that he wrote his books himself in Greek, but was sufficiently inexpert that he groped for the right word or phrase constantly, and probably needed coaches to help him out, resulting in a manuscript that did not really say what he meant; instead it gave the nearest Greek equivalent of what he meant. The other, more likely possibility, in my opinion, is similar to that given by the translator for the Penguin Classics[4] — who, all the same, speaks with undue surety of what we know nothing about for certain. However, based on the style of the Greek text, which is heavy-handedly literary, dull, formal, wordy, and laden with classical references and quotations, it is extremely unlikely that Josephus wrote them himself. Although he just barely might have had the huge Greek vocabulary necessary, we cannot imagine that he would have known Homer, Aeschylus, and Euripides so thoroughly as to quote them all the time.

Probably, then, he dictated his books to skilled scribes,[5] as was indeed the custom everywhere in those days except among Jews (the only Old World people who were universally literate). He might have worked from Aramaic notes, but would have dictated either in Greek or in Latin (which he

---

4 Josephus: *The Jewish War*.

5 Williamson takes it for granted that Josephus did this, though I wonder how he knows. I don't think he was there to see.

would have known far better than Greek), since gentile scribes would not know Aramaic. The scribes would then, following custom, write down whatever he said, and later "work it up." That is, they would copy over Josephus' halting, fumbling version (remember that Greek and Latin were both foreign languages for him), and rewrite it until they set down a polished, consciously literary version, full of ornamental phrases and quotations from the classics.[6]

This would explain the extremely un-Jewish feel of the text, and also its horrendously bad literary style. It would also explain another curious feature, namely that all Jewish weights, measures, and coinages are replaced haphazardly by the nearest Greek term, without regard for accuracy. Thus *dinar* becomes *stater*, although the monetary values are quite different, simply because *stater* was the closest approximation. And *maneh* becomes *drachma*, not at all the same weight, but it sounds more or less suitable. Obviously, any detailed analysis, say of market values or of a building's dimensions, will come out wildly wrong.[7] Just as obviously, Josephus didn't care. Or else his scribes didn't care, and he didn't care what they wrote — or was unable to read it. We truly don't know how well he spoke Greek.

More fundamentally, Jewish concepts and customs are substituted on the same principle by the nearest Greek equivalent, even though "nearest" in this context can only mean "worlds apart." This gives the text its strongly idola-

---

6 Bad taste has been common in all ages, and expert scribes in Roman days were men of great book-learning and a total lack of imagination: faithful drudges who would accomplish the project no matter how difficult, and who didn't care what the results were as long as the book was finished. Scholarly fidelity to facts was a concept unknown to them.

7 Whiston's solemnly methodical attempt to establish a "genuine scale of ancient Hebrew weights and measures" on the basis of Josephus' account ("certainly more to be believed than the *Rabbins*") makes for hysterical reading, and incidentally provides further evidence that Whiston was not quite right in the head.

trous flavor, and dooms any research into "Jewish thought and practice in Roman times," based on Josephus, to frustration.

Picture how it might have been when Josephus dictated his early chapters: he is attempting to describe, in only fairly good Latin, all about Jewish daily life and belief to a group of scribes who have not the faintest idea what he is talking about. Not only that, they must write it all down in Greek, which of course has no words (any more than Latin does) for Jewish concepts. No doubt they did not even bother shrugging. They simply wrote whatever sounded good in Greek, using the terminology that was familiar to them and adding lots of ornamental phrases, never sparing a moment to wonder what this weird Jew's babbling really meant. We cannot say for sure that this is how the books were actually written, but this is the impression that they give. If the impression is correct, all conclusions about Jewish matters on their basis is worthless.

A further consideration is that we who must read Josephus in English are reading a translation of a translation. The Greek itself was a "translation" from Josephus' mental Aramaic (and probably made through Latin, too), and the English is a translation from the Greek. Worse yet, except for *The Jewish War* the only English version available is Whiston's. This peculiar gentleman knew Greek excellently, but had very bad taste as a translator (it is said that he never used two words when six would do). He also was a crackpot — for a single example, he was convinced that Josephus was an early Christian bishop. The accuracy of his text is thus open to question, to say the least. Williamson plainly labels it grossly inaccurate.

So what do we have? A book written by a traitor, rewritten by gentiles, and translated by an eccentric. This is why I have never considered Josephus a serious historian, and why I think one should approach his histories with caution and a strong critical sense.

Further puzzles about the Second Temple period await us in the Books of Maccabees, our main source of information about Chanukkah and the early Hasmonean period. It's hard to say anything at all definite on this subject, but I will summarize what I think is reasonable to assume and what is likely to be true.

One confusing detail is that there are not one but four Books of Maccabees, all definitely by different authors.[8] 3 and 4 Maccabees are not germane here, since they have nothing to do with Chanukkah and the authors are of questionable *kashrus*. In any case, only 1 and 2 Maccabees are liable to impress anyone as being historical accounts. (3 and 4 are obviously tracts, aimed at putting over a certain lesson.)

But what are 1 and 2 Maccabees? The question is complicated by the uncertainty of the texts' sources. The only source for the Books of Maccabees is the Septuagint; but Maccabees belongs to the Apocryphal books, and most manuscripts of the Septuagint do not contain the Apocrypha at all. Worse yet, the Septuagint that we see today is very far from the text made by the seventy elders for Ptolemy of Egypt. For example, none of the intentional mistranslations they introduced survive today. By Origen's time (2d century CE) there were widely varying texts, and even after his editing efforts the original Hebrew was repeatedly consulted in later times in order to correct the Greek. Furthermore, the oldest surviving manuscripts of the Septuagint are not very reliable, and they all differ from each other somewhat.

Still, the varying texts of Maccabees that we see today are all essentially the same book, or books. The text, in other words, is good enough for us to get the gist of the story.

However, 1 and 2 Maccabees could not have been written by the same man, and probably were not written in the same

---

8 By "definitely" I mean that any reasonable man would agree, after a thorough reading, that it is most likely so; I don't mean that we can prove it, or that there is anything to go on but the internal evidence of the texts.

time. 1 Maccabees is a sober, if very moralistic, account of history, written in a plain, direct, matter-of-fact style. 2 Maccabees is a passionately poetic, dramatic account, full of windy phrases and lengthy exclamations, all just as Hellenistic taste decreed. That is, 1 Maccabees is the sort of thing an old-fashioned, kosher Jew would have written, and it might even have been written in Hebrew originally; it certainly reads like a translation from Hebrew. Whereas 2 Maccabees is definitely a Greek book: in style, in phrasing, and also in the liberal use of "embellishments" to the main story. In plain words, 2 Maccabees is full of fairy tales — long-winded miracles, signs, portents, apparitions, and visions — such that no sensible person would believe more than a quarter of it, if that much.

1 Maccabees reads far more like what a historian is looking for. But however reliable it may look at first glance, we still must ask whether the story it tells is actually true. Is all of it true, or some of it, or only a few bits of it? There is no way we can say. The text more or less corresponds to what we are taught in *cheder*, but we ought to stop and ask whether *cheder rebbes* have been influenced by the Books of Maccabees. The question is a legitimate one, or so I think.

To complicate matters further, some of our favorite Chanukkah stories, like Chanah and her seven sons and the defeat of Nikanor, appear in 2 Maccabees but not in 1 Maccabees. Does that mean that 2 Maccabees is more historically correct than 1 Maccabees? Does it mean that the rest of 2 Maccabees is also true? I would suggest not: to my mind it is more reasonable to say that the author of 1 Maccabees was interested in writing a sober *and brief* factual account of the Greek War period, whereas the author of 2 Maccabees had a good ear for a story and wanted to write a rousing piece of literature that would be more or less factual — a "historical novel," essentially. Such things tend to end up less, rather than more, factual.⁹

Among gentile scholars the tendency is to accept such situations as this one with a shrug and the old saying, *Se non è vero è ben trovato,* If it isn't true it's at least a good story. For Torah this will not do, but, unfortunately, we simply do not have the means to determine the facts here.

Nor is 1 Maccabees less troublesome than 2 Maccabees, if one takes the time to look into it. The version of events that it gives is not always what we are accustomed to, and by no means can all of the differences be ascribed to translator's inaccuracies. The author sounds very pious, but he makes no mention of the miracle of the *menorah,* and he makes it sound as if the people chose Shimon Maccabi to be their leader and governor, rather than that the Sanhedrin appointed him king. Then again, the book altogether has a biblical feel to it rather than a Torah-true feel, making one wonder if the author was a Sadducee or had leanings that way. But we don't know who he was; there is in fact no evidence at all to indicate his identity. Some scholars pretend that he was "probably the court historian of John Hyrcanus, son of Simon Maccabee"; but this is nothing but words. We in fact do not know whether Yochanan Horkenos even had a court historian, much less what such a man might have written. As we have seen, the wars of the next couple of centuries left almost nothing to tell us about those times.

A more subtle problem is that we don't know *why* this author wrote his book, nor for what audience. The audience one aims at dictates how much he will say, and how he will say it;¹⁰ and the reason for writing dictates what slant he will

---

9 The fact that the author claims to draw on "the writings of Jason of Cyrene" is no reassurance, since we know nothing whatever of Jason or his writings, or even whether he existed. So we cannot check up on this author to see whether he quoted responsibly, any more than we can examine Jason's writings to see whether they have any truth in them.

10 For example, an intended audience of gentiles, who would be unacquainted with the Oral Law, might account for the biblical feel of the text

give his material. We know none of this, so we cannot determine the accuracy, and the integrity, of what we read.

Added to this is the fact that, as with Josephus, we are dealing here with a translation of a translation. More precisely, 2 Maccabees was, as far as any reasonable man can judge, written in Greek; but 1 Maccabees has the feel of a Hebrew book, indicating that the author either was thinking in Hebrew while he wrote in Greek, or wrote in Hebrew originally and his text is lost. (Origen says that he had heard of a Hebrew original of 1 Maccabees, and he had no reason that I know of to lie about it, but "I have heard" is not the same as "I have seen.")

It seems to me, all in all, that one can only use his good sense and a lot of guesswork in dealing with 1 and 2 Maccabees. The fact that we have nothing better to read does not mean that these books are worth reading; the fact that they agree more or less with what we understand to have happened does not mean that they are accurate. Yet at the same time we have no reason to reject at least 1 Maccabees out of hand. For what it is worth, the author seems a reasonable man, and gives a straightforward impression.[11]

It would be worthwhile for someone to make a detailed comparison of 1 and 2 Maccabees with the text of *Megillat Antiochos,* which can be found in *Siddur Otzar HaTefillos.* The fact that this *"megillah"* was once read in a Jewish community does not give it an automatic *kashrus* certificate, but presumably the people had good sense, and their text just might represent a summary of what was once known to be true about the Maccabean story. Whoever is able, and has the time, to weigh the evidence in this case would be doing a mitzvah.

---

without calling the author's personal *kashrus* into question.

11 Though this might mean only that he was a skilled trickster. "An honest face is the con man's stock-in-trade," we say.

How much, then, do we know about the Second Temple period? The answer depends on what you mean by "knowing." The few things that Chazal tell us we know are true; but they didn't say much, since, as we said, Chazal's interest was in teaching us Torah, not recording history. In addition we can surmise a good deal, but this is not the same thing as truly knowing. We can examine textual evidence and conclude that this historical text or that one is more or less accurate; and we can deduce, using various logical methods, which parts of each text are likely to be more reliable and which less. Such guesswork, though, is never certain — these are surmises, not facts. So, although the past is not a closed book to us, it is a book we can only read part of.

CHANUKAH DATE LINE

Chronology From the Destruction of the First Temple to the Destruction of the Second Temple

3320	440 B.C.E	Nebuchadnezzar ascends to the throne of Babylon
3338	422 B.C.E	**Nebuchadnezzar destroys the First Temple; Beginning of Babylon Exile**
3389	371 B.C.E	Belshazzar assassinated; Babylon falls to Medes and Persians
3391	369 B.C.E	Darius dies; Cyrus succeeds him and proclaims right of Jews to return to Eretz Yisrael; Daniel leaves royal service
3394	366 B.C.E	Achashverosh becomes king
3405	355 B.C.E	**Miracle of Purim**
3407	353 B.C.E	Darius (son of Esther) succeeds Achashverosh
3408	352 B.C.E	**Darius permits building of Second Temple**
3442	319 B.C.E	**Beginning of Greek Era; Alexander conquers Persian Empire; Alexander dies at age 33 and his generals divide his empire**
3448	313 B.C.E	Egyptian Ptolemaic (Greek) dynasty rules Eretz Yisrael
3562	199 B.C.E	Antiochus III the Great, scion of the Seleucid (Greek) dynasty and ruler of Syria wrests Eretz Yisrael from Egypt
3571	190 B.C.E	Rome defeats Antiochus III at Magnesia
3586	175 B.C.E	Antiochus IV reigns
3594	168 B.C.E	Desecration of Temple by Antiochus IV

3597	165 B.C.E	**Conquest of Temple by Hasmoneans; The miracle of Chanukah (25 Kislev)**
3598	163 B.C.E	Antiochus IV dies
3599	162 B.C.E	His son, Antiochus V besieges Jerusalem
3600	161 B.C.E	Demetrius I (son of Seleucus IV) rules; Alcimus appointed Kohen Gadol; defeat and death of Syrian general Nikanor (13 Adar)
3601	160 B.C.E	Yehuda killed in battle; Yehonoson elected leader of the Jewish rebellion
3602	159 B.C.E	Alcimus dies
3609	152 B.C.E	Alexander (Balas) I, alleged son of Antiochus IV, contests Demetrius' I rule; both recognize Yehonoson as Kohen Gadol
3610	151 B.C.E	Alexander I rules
3619	142 B.C.E	Tryphon tricks Yehonoson and kills him; Shimon takes over Kehunah Gedolah; proclaims himself 'Prince of the Jews'
3621	140 B.C.E	Sanhedrin and the People proclaim Shimon 'Prince of the Jews' (18 Elul)
3621-3725	140-36 B.C.E	Rule of the Hasmonean dynasty (Shimon, Yochanan Hyrkanos, Yehuda Aristobulus, Alexander Yannai, Queen Alexandra, Hyrkanos and Aristobulus)
3698	63 B.C.E	Roman consul Pompei conquers Jerusalem
3725-3828	36 B.C.E.-68 C.E.	**Rule of Herodian dynasty and Roman governors (Herod, Archelaus, Roman governors, Agrippa I, Roman governors)**
3828	68 C.E	**Destruction of Second Temple by Romans**

*The dates in this table pertaining to the events of Chanukah (3585-3621) have been taken from I Maccabees and converted into Creation and Common Era dates.

This chronology is based on various ArtScroll books.

רָעוֹת שָׂבְעָה נַפְשִׁי. בְּיָגוֹן כֹּחִי כִּלָּה. חַיַּי מֵרְרוּ בְקֹשִׁי. בְּשִׁעְבּוּד
מַלְכוּת עֶגְלָה. וּבְיָדוֹ הַגְּדוֹלָה. הוֹצִיא אֶת הַסְּגֻלָּה. חֵיל פַּרְעֹה וְכָל
זַרְעוֹ. יָרְדוּ כְּאֶבֶן בִּמְצוּלָה:

דְּבִיר קָדְשׁוֹ הֱבִיאַנִי. וְגַם שָׁם לֹא שָׁקַטְתִּי. וּבָא נוֹגֵשׂ וְהִגְלַנִי. כִּי
זָרִים עָבַדְתִּי. וְיֵין רַעַל מָסַכְתִּי. כִּמְעַט שֶׁעָבַרְתִּי. קֵץ בָּבֶל. זְרֻבָּבֶל.
לְקֵץ שִׁבְעִים נוֹשָׁעְתִּי:

כְּרוֹת קוֹמַת בְּרוֹשׁ. בִּקֵּשׁ אֲגָגִי בֶּן הַמְּדָתָא. וְנִהְיְתָה לוֹ לְפַח
וּלְמוֹקֵשׁ. וְגַאֲוָתוֹ נִשְׁבָּתָה. רֹאשׁ יְמִינִי נִשֵּׂאתָ. וְאוֹיֵב שְׁמוֹ מָחִיתָ.
רֹב בָּנָיו. וְקִנְיָנָיו. עַל הָעֵץ תָּלִיתָ:

יְוָנִים נִקְבְּצוּ עָלַי. אֲזַי בִּימֵי חַשְׁמַנִּים. וּפָרְצוּ חוֹמוֹת מִגְדָּלַי. וְטִמְּאוּ
כָּל הַשְּׁמָנִים. וּמִנּוֹתַר קַנְקַנִּים. נַעֲשָׂה נֵס לַשּׁוֹשַׁנִּים. בְּנֵי בִינָה. יְמֵי
שְׁמוֹנָה. קָבְעוּ שִׁיר וּרְנָנִים:

חֲשׂוֹף זְרוֹעַ קָדְשֶׁךָ. וְקָרֵב קֵץ הַיְשׁוּעָה. נְקֹם נִקְמַת דַּם עֲבָדֶיךָ.
מֵאֻמָּה הָרְשָׁעָה. כִּי אָרְכָה לָנוּ הַיְשׁוּעָה. וְאֵין קֵץ לִימֵי הָרָעָה. דְּחֵה
אַדְמוֹן. בְּצֵל צַלְמוֹן. הָקֵם לָנוּ רוֹעֶה שִׁבְעָה:

אָנָּא בְכֹחַ גְּדֻלַּת יְמִינְךָ, תַּתִּיר צְרוּרָה: אב"ג ית"ץ
קַבֵּל רִנַּת עַמְּךָ, שַׂגְּבֵנוּ, טַהֲרֵנוּ, נוֹרָא: קר"ע שט"ן
נָא גִבּוֹר, דּוֹרְשֵׁי יִחוּדְךָ, כְּבָבַת שָׁמְרֵם: נג"ד יכ"ש
בָּרְכֵם טַהֲרֵם, רַחֲמֵי צִדְקָתְךָ תָּמִיד גָּמְלֵם: בט"ר צת"ג
חֲסִין קָדוֹשׁ, בְּרֹב טוּבְךָ נַהֵל עֲדָתֶךָ: חק"ב טנ"ע
יָחִיד גֵּאֶה, לְעַמְּךָ פְּנֵה, זוֹכְרֵי קְדֻשָּׁתֶךָ: יג"ל פז"ק
שַׁוְעָתֵנוּ קַבֵּל, וּשְׁמַע צַעֲקָתֵנוּ, יוֹדֵעַ תַּעֲלוּמוֹת: שק"ו צי"ת
בָּרוּךְ שֵׁם כְּבוֹד מַלְכוּתוֹ לְעוֹלָם וָעֶד

מִזְמוֹר שִׁיר, חֲנֻכַּת הַבַּיִת, לְדָוִד. אֲרוֹמִמְךָ ה', כִּי דִלִּיתָנִי, וְלֹא שִׂמַּחְתָּ אֹיְבַי לִי. ה' אֱלֹקָי, שִׁוַּעְתִּי
אֵלֶיךָ וַתִּרְפָּאֵנִי. ה' הֶעֱלִיתָ מִן שְׁאוֹל נַפְשִׁי, חִיִּיתַנִי מִיָּרְדִי בוֹר. זַמְּרוּ לַה' חֲסִידָיו, וְהוֹדוּ לְזֵכֶר
קָדְשׁוֹ. כִּי רֶגַע בְּאַפּוֹ, חַיִּים בִּרְצוֹנוֹ, בָּעֶרֶב יָלִין בֶּכִי, וְלַבֹּקֶר רִנָּה. וַאֲנִי אָמַרְתִּי בְשַׁלְוִי, בַּל אֶמּוֹט
לְעוֹלָם. ה', בִּרְצוֹנְךָ הֶעֱמַדְתָּה לְהַרְרִי עֹז, הִסְתַּרְתָּ פָנֶיךָ, הָיִיתִי נִבְהָל. אֵלֶיךָ ה' אֶקְרָא, וְאֶל ה'
אֶתְחַנָּן. מַה בֶּצַע בְּדָמִי, בְּרִדְתִּי אֶל שָׁחַת, הֲיוֹדְךָ עָפָר, הֲיַגִּיד אֲמִתֶּךָ. שְׁמַע ה' וְחָנֵּנִי, ה' הֱיֵה עֹזֵר
לִי. הָפַכְתָּ מִסְפְּדִי לְמָחוֹל לִי, פִּתַּחְתָּ שַׂקִּי, וַתְּאַזְּרֵנִי שִׂמְחָה. לְמַעַן יְזַמֶּרְךָ כָבוֹד וְלֹא יִדֹּם, ה' אֱלֹקַי
לְעוֹלָם אוֹדֶךָּ.

לַמְנַצֵּחַ בִּנְגִינֹת מִזְמוֹר שִׁיר: אֱלֹהִים יְחָנֵּנוּ וִיבָרְכֵנוּ יָאֵר פָּנָיו אִתָּנוּ סֶלָה: לָדַעַת בָּאָרֶץ דַּרְכֶּךָ בְּכָל
גּוֹיִם יְשׁוּעָתֶךָ: יוֹדוּךָ עַמִּים אֱלֹקִים יוֹדוּךָ עַמִּים כֻּלָּם: יִשְׂמְחוּ וִירַנְּנוּ לְאֻמִּים כִּי תִשְׁפֹּט עַמִּים
מִישֹׁר וּלְאֻמִּים בָּאָרֶץ תַּנְחֵם סֶלָה: יוֹדוּךָ עַמִּים אֱלֹקִים יוֹדוּךָ עַמִּים כֻּלָּם: אֶרֶץ נָתְנָה יְבוּלָהּ
יְבָרְכֵנוּ אֱלֹקִים אֱלֹקֵינוּ: יְבָרְכֵנוּ אֱלֹקִים וְיִירְאוּ אוֹתוֹ כָּל אַפְסֵי אָרֶץ:

סדר הדלקת נרות של חנוכה.

תפלה מהגה"ק ר' צבי אלימלך מדינוב זצוק"ל

לשם יחוד קודשא בריך הוא ושכינתיה בדחילו ורחימו ודחילו לייחד שם י"ה בו"ה ביחודא שלים בשם כל ישראל הנני מכון בהדלקת נר חנוכה לקיים מצות בוראי כאשר ציווני חכמינו ז"ל לתקן את שורשה במקום עליון: ובכן יהי רצון מלפניך ה' אלקינו ואלקי אבותינו שיהא חשוב ומקובל ומרצה לפניך מצות הדלקת נר חנוכה כאלו כוונתי כל הכוונות שכוונו הכהנים משרתיך השם בעת אשר הערו נפשם בשביל כבוד שמך הגדול הגבור והנורא. ואתה ברחמיך הרבים עורר עליהם נצחך לנצח את אויביהם ולנצח על מלאכת בית ה' והנני עושה על דעתם ועל כוונתם ועל דעת כל הצדיקים והחסידים שהיו באותו הדור שהשפעת להם נסיך וזכו לאור באור החיים ועל דעת כל הצדיקים והחסידים שבדורותינו ועפ"י כפיהם ועשיתי כעשייתם ובזכות המצוה הזאת תזכנו לנצח את אויבינו ולנצח על מלאכת בית ה' ונגלה כבוד מלכותך עלינו מהרה ולא ימוש התורה מפינו ומפי זרענו ומפי זרע זרענו מעתה ועד עולם ונזכה לבנים תלמידי חכמים אמן כן יהי רצון:

קדשנו במצותיך ותן חלקנו בתורתך שבענו מטובך ושמח נפשנו בישועתך וטהר לבנו לעבדך באמת מלוך על כל העולם כלו בכבודך והנשא על כל הארץ ביקרך והופע בהדר גאון עזך על כל יושבי תבל ארצך וידע כל פעול כי אתה פעלתו ויבין כל יצור כי אתה יצרתו ויאמר כל אשר נשמה באפו (נר חנוכ"ה) ה' אלקי ישראל מלך ומלכותו בכל משלה: אמן נצח סלה ועד:

בָּרוּךְ אַתָּה ה' אֱלֹקֵינוּ מֶלֶךְ הָעוֹלָם אֲשֶׁר קִדְּשָׁנוּ בְּמִצְוֹתָיו וְצִוָּנוּ לְהַדְלִיק נֵר חֲנֻכָּה:

בָּרוּךְ אַתָּה ה' אֱלֹקֵינוּ מֶלֶךְ הָעוֹלָם שֶׁעָשָׂה נִסִּים לַאֲבוֹתֵינוּ בַּיָּמִים הָהֵם בַּזְּמַן הַזֶּה:

בָּרוּךְ אַתָּה ה' אֱלֹקֵינוּ מֶלֶךְ הָעוֹלָם שֶׁהֶחֱיָנוּ וְקִיְּמָנוּ וְהִגִּיעָנוּ לַזְּמַן הַזֶּה:

הַנֵּרוֹת הַלָּלוּ אֲנַחְנוּ מַדְלִיקִים עַל הַנִּסִּים וְעַל הַנִּפְלָאוֹת וְעַל הַתְּשׁוּעוֹת וְעַל הַמִּלְחָמוֹת שֶׁעָשִׂיתָ לַאֲבוֹתֵינוּ בַּיָּמִים הָהֵם בַּזְּמַן הַזֶּה עַל יְדֵי כֹּהֲנֶיךָ הַקְּדוֹשִׁים. וְכָל שְׁמוֹנַת יְמֵי חֲנֻכָּה הַנֵּרוֹת הַלָּלוּ קֹדֶשׁ הֵם וְאֵין לָנוּ רְשׁוּת לְהִשְׁתַּמֵּשׁ בָּהֶם אֶלָּא לִרְאוֹתָם בִּלְבַד כְּדֵי לְהוֹדוֹת וּלְהַלֵּל לְשִׁמְךָ הַגָּדוֹל עַל נִסֶּיךָ וְעַל נִפְלְאוֹתֶיךָ וְעַל יְשׁוּעָתֶךָ:

מָעוֹז צוּר יְשׁוּעָתִי. לְךָ נָאֶה לְשַׁבֵּחַ. תִּכּוֹן בֵּית תְּפִלָּתִי. וְשָׁם תּוֹדָה נְזַבֵּחַ. לְעֵת תָּכִין מַטְבֵּחַ. מִצָּר הַמְנַבֵּחַ. אָז אֶגְמוֹר. בְּשִׁיר מִזְמוֹר. חֲנֻכַּת הַמִּזְבֵּחַ:

BOOKS BY THE SAME AUTHOR

Living Beyond Time: The Mystery and Meaning of the Jewish Festivals. 446 pages. Sha'ar Press. $24.99

The Sacred Trust: Love, Dating and Marriage: The Jewish View. 125 pages. NCSY/OU (ArtScroll). $14.99

Purim In A New Light: Mystery, Grandeur and Depth, as revealed through the writings of Rabbi Yitzchak Hutner (Pachad Yitzchak). 243 pages. David Dov Publications. $23.95

Chanukah In A New Light: Grandeur, Heroism and Depth, as revealed through the writings of Rabbi Yitzchak Hutner (Pachad Yitzchak). 240 pages. David Dov Publications. $23.95

Hidden Lights: Chanukah and the Jewish/Greek Conflict. 291 pages. David Dov Publications. $23.95

These books are available at your local Jewish book store, or can be purchased from The David Dov Foundation, 603 Twin Oaks Drive, Lakewood, NJ 08701, by mail. There is no additional cost for postage or delivery. Please allow three weeks for delivery.